Passing your
Driving Tests

Passing your
Driving Tests

*How to be prepared
and feel confident of success*

ANGELA OATRIDGE
2nd edition

How To Books

Published by How To Books Ltd,
3 Newtec Place, Magdalen Road,
Oxford OX4 1RE. United Kingdom.
Tel: (01865) 793806. Fax: (01865) 248780.
email: info@howtobooks.co.uk
http://www.howtobooks.co.uk

First edition 1998.
Second edition 1999.
Reprinted 1999.

British Library Cataloguing in Publication Data.
A catalogue record for this book is available from
the British Library.

Cover design by Shireen Nathoo Design
Cover image PhotoDisc
Cartoons by Mike Flanagan

Produced for How To Books by Deer Park Productions
Typeset by PDQ Typesetting, Stoke-on-Trent, Staffs.
Printed and bound by Cromwell Press, Trowbridge, Wiltshire

NOTE: The material contained in this book is set out in good
faith for general guidance and no liability can be accepted
for loss or expense incurred as a result of relying in particular
circumstances on statements made in the book. Laws and
regulations are complex and liable to change, and readers should
check the current position with the relevant authorities before
making personal arrangements.

Contents

List of illustrations   8

Preface   9

1   Understanding the importance of the driving tests   11

Ensuring safety on the roads   11
Demonstrating your knowledge of *The Highway Code*   13
Showing knowledge of basic technical and safety skills   15
Checklist   17
Questions and answers   17
Case studies   18
Discussion points   20

2   Taking the theory test   21

Preparing for the theory test   21
Having the right attitude   23
Knowing what to take to the theory test   23
Reading and understanding the theory test paper   24
Coping with complex questions   29
Checking your answers   29
Checklist   30
Questions and answers   30
Case studies   31
Discussion points   32

3   Preparing for the practical test   33

Ensuring you are ready for the practical test   33
Having the right type of instruction   33
Having a suitable vehicle   34
Checking your eyesight is up to standard   35
Checking that you have all the correct paperwork   35
Checklist   36
Questions and answers   36
Case studies   37
Discussion points   39

4   Coping on the day of your practical test   40

Having a positive attitude   40
Presenting a good appearance   41
Ensuring you have the necessary paperwork   42
Allowing time for parking   42
Checklist   43
Questions and answers   43
Case studies   43
Discussion points   46

5   Meeting your examiner   47

Controlling your nerves   47
Leading the way to your vehicle   48
Reading a number plate correctly   48
Remembering your five cockpit checks   49
Checklist   50
Questions and answers   50
Case studies   51
Discussion points   54

6   Moving off smoothly   55

Starting the engine   55
Moving away from the kerb   55
Balancing your clutch and accelerator   56
Checklist   57
Questions and answers   57
Case studies   58
Discussion points   60

7   Reading the road ahead   61

Understanding the importance of forward planning   61
Acting on signs and signals   62
Being in the right gear at the right time   64
Observing what is happening all around you   65
Checklist   66
Questions and answers   66
Case studies   67
Discussion points   68

8   Doing the manoeuvres correctly   69

Understanding the importance of clutch control   69
Being extra observant at all times   70
Knowing what to do if your manoeuvring is going wrong   70
Understanding the importance of positive thinking   72
Checklist   73

Questions and answers   73
Case studies   75
Discussion points   76

9   Understanding the examiner's requests   **77**

Following the road ahead   77
Selecting a safe place to stop   79
Moving off when safe to do so   80
Doing the emergency stop   80
Checklist   81
Questions and answers   82
Case studies   82
Discussion points   84

10   Thinking positively at all times   **85**

Overcoming common problems   85
Breathing correctly to help ease nervous tension   86
Observing other road users at all times   87
Obeying the rules of *The Highway Code*   88
Having confidence to take charge inside your vehicle   89
Checklist   90
Questions and answers   91
Case studies   92
Discussion points   93

11   Coping with hazards   **94**

Knowing what to do when encountering unexpected hazards   94
Dealing with inclement weather   96
Feeling too nervous to carry on   97
Checklist   98
Questions and answers   98
Case studies   100
Discussion points   101

12   Hearing the results of your tests   **102**

Receiving the results of the theory test   102
Listening to what the examiner tells you   102
Knowing what to do after your driving test   105
Checklist   106
Questions and answers   106
Case studies   107
Discussion points   109

Glossary   110
Further reading   111
Index   112

List of Illustrations

1. The route to being a good driver   16

2. Front cover of the DSA theory test   26

3. Examples of questions you may be asked, with the correct   28
   answers

4. Correcting your answer   30

5. The five cockpit checks   50

6. The see-saw movement of clutch and accelerator   57

7. Understanding the sequence of traffic lights   62

8. Turning in a road lined with trees   74

9. Pulling out when parked cars obscure your view   96

10. Driving test report   104

Preface

Driving tests cause more tension, more sleepless nights and more loss of confidence than perhaps any other test you are likely to take. Many people fail through sheer nerves, and not because they are incompetent drivers. During my time as a driving instructor on the Continent I accompanied learner drivers on their tests, as was the practice. On many occasions I witnessed perfectly able drivers behave out of character due to stress.

1999 has been the year of major changes in the practical driving test, including the introduction of a slightly longer test to enable candidates to have time to drive on faster roads and dual carriageways when available. January 2000 will see the introduction of computerized testing for the theory test which will enable candidates to receive their results immediately.

Passing Your Driving Tests has already proved invaluable to the many people who bought the first edition. However, new laws, regulations and test requirements are forever changing. The importance of correct instruction with the aid of a professional fully qualified ADI is even more important today, not only at the initial stages but also to help and advise you on the big day itself.

This book aims to help you through the last few weeks before you sit both theory and practical tests. It will help you understand what is expected from you and show how you can prepare thoroughly, so that you are as confident as possible on both occasions. There is also advice on how to relax during the actual tests, particularly the practical test where your every move is under scrutiny. If things do start to go wrong it's how you cope that matters. During the following pages I will help you prepare for those situations so that you keep a clear head and don't panic.

ACKNOWLEDGEMENTS

Crown copyright material reproduced under licence from the Controller of HMSO and the Driving Standards Agency.

Angela Oatridge

1
Understanding the Importance of the Driving Tests

ENSURING SAFETY ON THE ROADS

Being able to drive well is one of the major skills needed to be able to cope with today's fast moving world. However, the actual driving tests are a huge hurdle for most learner drivers. Many people anticipate the day of their driving test with more dread than a visit to the dentist or a minor operation. It is also a major topic of conversation whenever drivers are gathered together. Tall stories are told about quota of passes, examiners to avoid, and many more tales which fill the poor candidate with dread as D-day approaches.

Driving tests have only one aim and that is simply to ensure that the candidate:

- is **competent** to drive without danger
- shows **due care and consideration** to other road users and
- displays a **responsible attitude** while driving.

So let's start off with clarifying exactly what the driving tests require.

The theory test
The theory test is designed to ensure that new drivers:

- have a broad spread of driving knowledge
- understand the importance of driving skills.

The reading and study involved in the preparation for the theory test also help the potential driver to:

- prepare for the practical test
- cope with the ever increasing volume of traffic on today's roads
- understand the rules as laid out in *The Highway Code*
- have the correct attitude to driving.

The practical driving test
Once you have passed the theory test you will be able to take your

11

practical driving test. Before considering taking your practical driving test, remember:

- driving is a skill for life
- you must have plenty of practice.

The three other important factors in your training for a lifetime of safe driving are:

1. Being taught by a good driving instructor.
2. Understanding the importance of following the rules as laid down in *The Highway Code*.
3. Realising that, however good your instructor is, you are responsible for managing your own rate of learning.

Choose your instructor carefully
It is advisable to have lessons with a **qualified** driving instructor. A good driving instructor:

- explains, not blames, when you make a mistake
- doesn't shout
- shows patience, tolerance and understanding at all times.

Your driving lessons should be:

- informative
- well organised
- enjoyable.

If you feel your instructor does not suit you, find another one. Always remember that what is suitable for one person is not necessarily suitable for everyone. Even the best driving instructors sometimes come across people who are best taught by someone else.

During the initial stage of driving it is best to have a fully qualified driving instructor who displays the ADI sticker in the window. Although many people feel that perhaps it is better to have the basic skills taught by friends or family, thus saving money, bad or incorrect instruction at the initial stage can result in hours of extra tuition to correct faults which may have become routine to the learner. Fully qualified instructors have studied and taken numerous tests, and therefore:

- understand the importance of correct instruction at the initial stage

- are able to explain clearly each stage in a way that can be understood.

> Remember we all prefer to write on a clean sheet of paper rather than have to use one which requires a lot of rubbing out first.

DEMONSTRATING YOUR KNOWLEDGE OF *THE HIGHWAY CODE*

It is very important that you have not only read the current edition of *The Highway Code* but understand the rules and advice given in it. Throughout your practical test the examiner will be:

- observing your reaction to other road users' signals and actions
- noting your ability to 'read the road'
- seeing how you react to road signs.

Ensure that your copy of *The Highway Code* is the latest edition as the law is always changing and therefore it has to be updated regularly.

Reading the road

The ability to **read the road** is perhaps one of the major skills of a good driver. It involves:

- looking well ahead while driving

- knowing what is happening on all four sides of the car

- anticipating the actions of other road users

- observing all traffic signs and reacting accordingly

- noting the state of the surface of the road

- planning well ahead for anticipated dangers

- using speed correctly.

Observing traffic signs

Traffic signs cost a great deal of money to produce, therefore it is always worth remembering that they are there to help road users and to keep down the accident rate. Traffic signs can be a matter of life and death if ignored or read incorrectly.

As a driver it is vitally important that you always:

- observe all road signs

- understand what the sign means

- know what you are supposed to do and
- act accordingly.

It is also very important to understand the meanings of all the different road markings:

- box junctions with their crisscross of yellow lines
- yellow lines at the side of the road
- red, yellow and green reflective studs
- stop and give way lines at road junctions
- different lengths and types of white lines along the road.

The golden rule is to remember the more paint used the greater the hazard.

Anticipating the actions of other road users
The **observation** and **anticipation** of the actions of other road users, whether pedestrians, cyclists or other vehicles, is perhaps the secret of good driving. A good driver is therefore always:

- looking well ahead to see not only what the vehicle in front is doing but also the vehicles further ahead

- observing if there are children nearby, or people likely to step into the road

- aware of any pedal cyclists who may be passing on the inside as you slow down

- aware of the dangers of parked cars:
  – doors may open
  – children may dash out between cars
  – mothers with prams may push the pram ahead to gain better vision
  – vehicles may move out without signalling.

The golden rule in observation and anticipating is **never drive too close to the vehicle in front of you** – you will then have a far clearer picture of what is happening well ahead, and have more time to act on what you see.

SHOWING KNOWLEDGE OF BASIC TECHNICAL AND SAFETY SKILLS

You are not expected to be a motor engineer. However, it is important that you know and understand the importance of:

- correct tyre pressure
- catalytic converters
- having a good depth of tread on tyres
- wearing the correct footwear
- head rests
- safety equipment
- keeping a safe distance from the vehicle in front
- spotting when your shock absorbers are worn
- braking smoothly.

Besides these you should also be aware of:

- stopping distances
- how driving is affected by different road surfaces and weather conditions
- using your foot controls smoothly.

You should also know what to do in the event of:

- skidding
- having an accident.

An understanding of these is all part of what is required in modern day driving, together with a knowledge of:

- what affects the stability of a vehicle
- how to load a vehicle correctly
- towing regulations.

Acquiring a skill for life

The amount of study required to take a driving test today may seem rather daunting, but remember you are studying a skill for life which, if studied and practised correctly, will lead to a relatively accident-free lifetime.

Driving tests are there to ensure that you:

- understand all aspects of driving safely
- demonstrate you are a fit and suitable person to be in charge of a vehicle

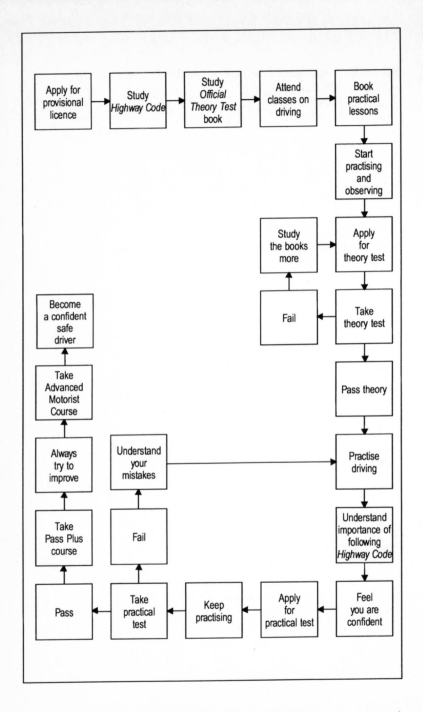

Fig. 1. The route to being a good driver.

- handle your vehicle safely.

CHECKLIST

You should now be aware of:

- why we have driving tests
- what is meant by demonstrating knowledge of *The Highway Code*
- the basic technical and safety knowledge required.

QUESTIONS AND ANSWERS

How many hours tuition do I need before taking my driving test? I have been told you need an hour for every year of your life – is this true?

Driving, like any other skill, is learned at different rates by different people. There is a lot to learn and understand in order to be a good driver on our very busy roads. Some people find it easy to handle a vehicle at the early stages of learning to drive; others find it takes a long time to learn how to use the controls smoothly. The more practice you have over a wide variety of different road and traffic conditions, the sooner you will be ready for your practical test. However, it helps if you read and understand all the relevant literature and have a chance to discuss the various points raised before attempting your theory test; you then have a better chance of passing this and are better prepared to pass the practical driving test.

The hours recommended are actually an hour and a half for each year of your life; however, this is a just a guideline – I personally have had pupils who have needed a lot less, and others a lot more. For example, I taught a 17-year-old nurse who took nearly two years to learn to drive, having one lesson a week. She was very nervous about driving, and used to forget things she had been taught. However, in her career she was working very hard and I understand she passed all her exams with flying colours. On the other hand I taught a 40-year-old housewife who had never driven before, but who had a natural aptitude for driving. She found it very easy to handle the controls and plan ahead. She passed her test first time, after only 16 hours tuition.

I have found that if you have any problems at work or at home it slows down the learning process, as the worry is always at the back of your mind while trying to learn a new skill.

I have been teaching my wife, who is Italian, to drive. She is very worried about her test as she can speak English but is not very good at reading it. Are the test papers available in Italian?

Test papers are available in some languages including Welsh, Gujerati, Hindi, Punjabi, Chinese, Bengali and Urdu, but not in Italian. When you apply for the theory test for your wife, if you make a note on the application form, or tell the operator if you phone, they will arrange for a member of staff to read the test to your wife on a one-to-one basis.

I am 68 years old and have recently been widowed. Although I have never taken the British driving test, I did have a licence when we lived in Malaya for ten years. When we returned to England my husband and I lived in London initially, then moved to the country. Although I started to have lessons on and off, I never got round to taking the test. I need to be able to drive as I live a long way from the nearest shops, but everyone says I am too old to take a test now. Is this true?

Providing you are in reasonably good health and your eyesight is up to the required standard, there is no reason for you not to start taking lessons again. I have taught many people over 60 to drive and have always found them very conscientious and eager to learn to drive safely and well. Normally people over 60 do take longer to learn, although as you have driven before you will find your skill at handling the controls will slowly return. You may find what will take time is learning to cope with the much busier and faster traffic on our roads today.

CASE STUDIES

Edward finds the answers
Edward was feeling very despondent – he had taken his theory test twice and had failed it both times.

'I really study everything,' he said, 'but I seem to forget it all!'

'Maybe you should have a few practical lessons,' his father suggested. 'Sometimes everything falls into place when you are actually driving. We will give you a course of ten lessons for Christmas, after which you might find that you can study the books and understand.'

Edward went to a driving school, and also practised with his parents. He found that once he was actually driving the theory part was so much easier to understand.

He took his theory test again and passed, and a month later he passed his practical test first time.

> Theory and practice work together and
> help when taking your tests.

Geoff realises he was a fool

Geoff learned to drive when he was 17 and had felt very confident when he took his test. However, he was so angry and disappointed when he was told he had failed that he told his friends he was not going to take the test again.

'They can keep their stupid driving tests,' he said. 'I'm not going to give them the satisfaction of failing me again. They only failed me because I was young.'

After a few years Geoff realised he needed to be able to drive, and had been stubborn and acted irrationally when he had failed his test at 17. He explained to his driving instructor, 'At the time I thought I was punishing the driving examiner for failing me, not giving him any work, which looking back seems very stupid as I only punished myself. Now I have to work twice as hard as not only is there more traffic around, but I also have to take a theory test.'

Geoff took a full course of lessons and passed his tests.

> If you fail your test practise a little more, and retake it as soon as possible. Remember the old saying, 'If at first you don't succeed, try, try, try again.'

Amy changes instructors

Amy was 30 when she had her first driving lesson. She was nervous and she found her instructor rather short tempered. After four lessons he told her that she would never make a driver, and suggested that it was a waste of good money for her to continue with lessons.

Amy was very upset, but had to agree that she was still having problems coordinating her feet, resulting too often in stalling. She was also aware that she had difficulty steering in a straight line, let alone round corners. She resigned herself to the fact that she was going to have to manage without driving for the rest of her life. However, as the weeks went by she felt that perhaps she could do it with the right instructor.

'After all', she thought, 'other people I know who are no smarter than I am seem to learn to drive and pass a test.'

She decided to find a new instructor, one who understood nervous people. After enquiring among her friends, she tried a different driving school which was recommended as being very patient with its learner drivers. She was amazed at the difference. She felt relaxed as everything was explained carefully. Her problems with steering and stalling were quickly rectified, and furthermore, at the end of the first lesson with her new instructor, she was informed that she had done very well. After six lessons Amy felt very confident and happy behind the wheel, and was more than delighted when her instructor informed her she had a natural feeling for driving, and would make an excellent driver: 'You are aware of dangers and you also look well ahead and plan accordingly.' Amy was able to pass her test first time after only 18 lessons with her new instructor.

> With the right instructor anyone can learn to drive. However, the number of lessons required depends on the individual.

DISCUSSION POINTS

1. Why do you think we in the UK have speed restrictions on motorways?

2. What do you think are the main attributes of a good driver?

3. Do you think the legal age of driving should be:

    - kept as 17 as it is now?
    - increased to 18?
    - decreased to 16?

2
Taking the Theory Test

PREPARING FOR THE THEORY TEST

The theory test is straightforward, but you do have to be prepared. The questions are designed to test your knowledge of road safety. The topics covered include:

- alertness
- attitude
- safety and your vehicle
- safety margins
- hazard awareness
- vulnerable road users
- other types of vehicle
- vehicle handling
- motorway rules
- rules of the road
- road and traffic signs
- documents
- accidents
- vehicle loading.

There are 35 questions on the paper and if you answer 30 or more correctly you will pass. You will have 40 minutes to complete the test.

As from January 2000 the theory test will be on a computer. Don't panic if you are not computer literate, the questions will remain the same and you will be carefully instructed how to display your answers. The big advantage will be that you will receive your results immediately.

Reading the right books
Before applying for the theory test you need to have studied the current edition of the following books:

- *The Official Theory Test for Car Drivers and Motorcyclists*
- *The Driving Test*

- *The Highway Code.*

It is also a good idea to read and study:

The Driving Manual

and if you are a motorcyclist:

- *The Motorcycling Manual.*

All these books are produced by the Driving Standards Agency (DSA) or the Department of Transport.

It is very important that you:

- understand the question
- know **why** an answer is correct, not just learn information parrot fashion.

The task of reading so many things, and trying to absorb so much information, can seem daunting at first. However, everything will gradually fall into place if you follow a simple five-step plan:

1. Read a little each day.
2. Ask your family or friends to test you on what you have read.
3. Watch the road ahead when you are a passenger in a car or bus and take note of how the driver acts on signs and situations.
4. Talk to your driving instructor about anything you find hard to understand.
5. Discuss with your friends who are learning to drive, or can drive, various aspects of the test and driving in general.

It can also help if you:

- attend classroom tuition
- obtain and watch the new video from The Driving Standards Agency entitled 'Making a Pass'
- study the CD Rom 'Driving Skills – Theory and Beyond'.

Remember
Driving is a skill for life, the more you

- read
- study
- understand

about

- the rules of the road
- the principles of good driving
- *The Highway Code*

the more chance you have of:

- passing your theory test
- passing your practical driving test
- enjoying a lifetime of safe driving.

HAVING THE RIGHT ATTITUDE

Any exam, interview or test you take is influenced by your attitude on the day. If you feel you will fail, you most likely will. It is therefore very important that you feel:

- relaxed
- confident
- prepared.

If you are feeling tired, angry or frustrated about anything, this will affect your performance.

Try to arrive in plenty of time for your tests so you can:

- go to the toilet, if required
- talk with other candidates
- sit and relax for five minutes
- have a final check on anything which is worrying you.

KNOWING WHAT TO TAKE TO THE THEORY TEST

Remember to have all the necessary documents with you. They are:

- your appointment card or booking number
- your driving licence which **must be signed**
- photo identity.

Photo identity

The DSA will need to confirm your identity, so will need to see some form of photographic evidence which also bears your signature. Any of the following would be acceptable as they bear both your photo and signature:

- your passport
- rail pass
- works identity card
- bus pass
- trade union card
- students union card
- cheque guarantee card or credit card (if it is one which carries a photo).

If you don't have any of the above don't worry! You can bring a photograph of yourself together with a signed statement that it's a true likeness of you, stating your full name. This must be signed by one of the following people:

- your approved driving instructor
- your doctor
- qualified teacher
- police officer
- minister of religion
- commissioned officer in Her Majesty's Forces
- Member of Parliament
- local authority councillor
- bank official
- barrister or solicitor
- Justice of the Peace
- an established civil servant.

It's also a good idea to bring some sweets as nerves can lead to a dry mouth.

Arriving at the test centre

The test centre staff will:

- check your documents
- make sure you are given the correct test paper (either car driver or motorcyclist) to complete.

If you have any books or papers with you the staff will ask you to surrender them until after the test.

    The test papers vary so it is very unlikely that you will be given the same paper as the person seated near you. If you have taken the test previously you are unlikely to get the same paper again.

READING AND UNDERSTANDING THE THEORY TEST PAPER

On the cover of your test paper there is a place for you to fill in:

- your surname
- first names
- booking reference number
- provisional licence number
- centre number
- date
- time.

You can start to fill in this part straight away. You will still have time to study the rest of the cover of the test paper, which will include two examples of questions and the correct way to mark them. You will also find a few sample questions on the cover – you will be given time to look at and attempt these before you start the test. **These questions are not part of the test**: however, you will find that trying to answer them correctly will help you get into the correct gear, mentally, for the actual test questions.

- Look at the questions carefully.
- Put a cross by the answer or answers you think are correct.

Some questions require more than one answer so carefully check you have given the required amount of answers. Figure 2 shows the front cover of the DSA theory test for drivers. Take time to familiarise yourself with it now, so that you will know what to expect on the day.

Starting the test
The staff will tell you when you can open the paper to start the test.

1.   Read each question carefully.
2.   Answer first the ones you are sure about.
3.   Note if the question requires one or more answers.

If you are not sure of an answer go on to the next question and come back to that one later. You may find another question which will provide the clue to the answer.

If a question includes a picture look at it carefully and think what you would be doing if you were driving the vehicle in question.

Remembering what the road signs mean
If you have a picture of **road signs** remember:

- **A red ring or circle** is a **no** sign. For example:
  - no overtaking
  - no parking
  - no going over 40 mph.

- **A blue ring or circle** gives a positive instruction:
  - you must turn right
  - you must go ahead
  - you must travel over 30 mph.

130013

THEORY TEST FOR DRIVERS

Surname

_____

First Names

_____

Booking Ref.   88

Pro. Licence No.

Centre No.   ENGLISH M.V.

	D	D	M	M	Y	Y	Y	Y
Date								

	H	H	M	M
Time				

GENERAL INSTRUCTIONS
1. For each question you must find the right answer(s) and mark an X in the box next to it.
2. Do not write any comments on your test paper.
3. Two examples have been done to show you how to mark your answers.
4. If you make a mistake cross out your original choice completely

   and mark your other choice as shown.

EXAMPLES

E1 — What MUST you have before you are allowed to drive in the UK?

Mark one answer

a ☒ A medical certificate

b ☒ A signed passport photograph

c ☒ A signed driving licence

d ☒ A copy of your birth certificate

E2 — Which TWO would help you to have a safe long journey?

Mark two answers

a ☒ Drive through the town centres

b ☒ Use a map to plan your journey

c ☒ Start out in plenty of time

d ☒ Set a time limit for your journey

e ☒ Avoid having breaks until near the end

P1 — This sign means

Mark one answer

a ☒ follow the tracks

b ☒ slippery road ahead

c ☒ change lanes

d ☒ vehicles liable to pass

P2 — You MUST stop when signalled to do so by which THREE of these?

Mark three answers

a ☒ A police officer

b ☒ A pedestrian

c ☒ A school crossing patrol

d ☒ A bus driver

e ☒ A red traffic light

P3 — What should you use the hard shoulder of a motorway for?

Mark one answer

a ☒ Stopping in an emergency

b ☒ Overtaking

c ☒ Stopping when you are tired

d ☒ Joining the motorway

P4 — What should the driver of the arrowed car do?

Mark one answer

a ☒ Pull out quickly

b ☒ Continue to wait for a safe gap in the traffic

c ☒ Continue to wait until the traffic lights change

d ☒ Gesture to the driver of the white car to ask her to stop

130013

Do not go on to the main test until you are told to do so.

Fig. 2. Front cover of the DSA theory test.

- **Triangles** warn of a danger ahead, for example:
  - crossroads ahead
  - uneven road ahead
  - steep hill ahead.

- **Rectangles** inform. The background colour denotes the type of route:
  - green on primary routes
  - white panels for local routes
  - brown panels for tourist information
  - blue panel for motorway routes and information.

Reading road signs is like reading a picture book. They are there to:

- help you read the road ahead
- warn you what to expect.

Therefore in any question where a road sign is shown, the picture will help you answer the question correctly.

The book *The Official Theory Test*:

- explains all the topics which will be covered in the question paper
- shows you the questions that might be asked, with the correct answers (see Figure 3).

You might be asked questions which do not appear in the book because test questions are always being reviewed, also the Department of Transport has to look at changes in the law and the results of customer feedback.

Coping with questions you can't answer
If you find a question where you are not sure of the answer or which you don't understand:

- don't panic
- move on to the next question immediately
- return to it when you have finished the questions you can answer.

When you go back to study these questions again:

- read each question carefully
- think logically.

If you still can't think of the correct answer:

- move on to another question

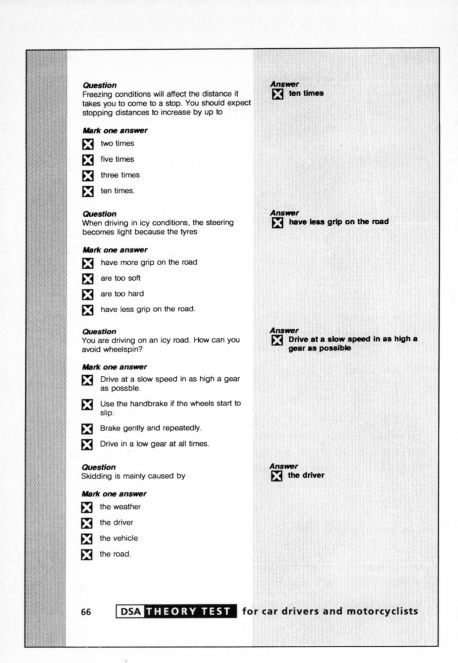

Question
Freezing conditions will affect the distance it takes you to come to a stop. You should expect stopping distances to increase by up to

Mark one answer

☒ two times

☒ five times

☒ three times

☒ ten times.

Answer
☒ ten times

Question
When driving in icy conditions, the steering becomes light because the tyres

Mark one answer

☒ have more grip on the road

☒ are too soft

☒ are too hard

☒ have less grip on the road.

Answer
☒ have less grip on the road

Question
You are driving on an icy road. How can you avoid wheelspin?

Mark one answer

☒ Drive at a slow speed in as high a gear as possble.

☒ Use the handbrake if the wheels start to slip.

☒ Brake gently and repeatedly.

☒ Drive in a low gear at all times.

Answer
☒ Drive at a slow speed in as high a gear as possible

Question
Skidding is mainly caused by

Mark one answer

☒ the weather

☒ the driver

☒ the vehicle

☒ the road.

Answer
☒ the driver

66 **DSA THEORY TEST** for car drivers and motorcyclists

Fig. 3. Examples of questions you may be asked, with the correct answers. (A page taken from *The Official Theory Test for Car Drivers and Motorcyclists* written and compiled by the Driving Standards Agency.)

- look for a clue in other questions.

Remember most questions are based on driving safely with consideration for other people, so think of this when looking at the question.

COPING WITH COMPLEX QUESTIONS

Some questions are more difficult to answer correctly because more than one answer seems to be correct. An example could be as follows:

Q.   You are driving along a narrow street with parked cars on both sides. Which two of the following are the main hazards which you should be aware of?

A.   ☐ lack of road markings
     ☐ oncoming traffic
     ☐ car doors opening suddenly
     ☐ road signs hidden by parked vehicles
     ☐ children running out from between vehicles
     ☐ cyclists riding along the road.

As you can see each is a hazard; however, if you read the question again carefully, they want the two *main hazards*.

- look at the six possible answers again
- think which hazards are going to be the easiest to cope with
- decide which is the main danger which may startle you, perhaps make you do an emergency stop.

The correct answers would be:

     ☒ car doors opening suddenly
     ☒ children running out from between vehicles.

Both these events could happen very suddenly and involve a hidden danger which requires extra:

- anticipation
- awareness
- observation
- control.

CHECKING YOUR ANSWERS

When you have answered all the questions check your answers

again. If you find you have answered incorrectly:

- cross out the box with the incorrect answer completely
- mark the box you think is correct (see Figure 4).

Remember you have 40 minutes to answer the questions.

Many people who fail the theory test do so because they have not read the question correctly. If you have any time left use it to check your answers again.

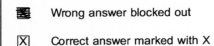

Fig. 4. Correcting your answer.

CHECKLIST

You should now feel more confident about:

- preparing for the theory test
- what you need to take with you
- what to do if you can't understand the question
- dealing with complex questions
- what you should do if you make a mistake in your answers.

QUESTIONS AND ANSWERS

My son is dyslexic and is worried that he may not be able to finish the paper in time?

If anyone has learning difficulties they will be given extra time to complete the question paper. It is important that you state your needs on the application form so that the necessary arrangements can be made.

My wife is Chinese and although she can speak quite good English, she cannot read or write well in the language. Can I come along with her to read the paper to her?

There is no need for you to come along as the paper is available in Chinese. Papers can also be supplied in Welsh, Bengali, Urdu,

Gujerati, Hindi and Punjabi. If a person cannot read or write any of the languages available then he or she can bring an approved translator with them. However, in this case you should inform the booking office beforehand.

I have had a full motorcycle licence for five years and now want to obtain a licence to drive a car. Do I have to take a theory test?

No, holders of a full licence for a motorcycle who wish to take a test to drive a car, or qualified car drivers who require a motorcycle licence, do not have to take the theory test.

CASE STUDIES

Jane forgets everything

Jane had worked hard studying for her theory test; as both a secretary and mother of three children she was used to coping with pressure. As she entered the room to take her test she felt confident. However, when she opened the paper she noticed a question which she could not answer. She suddenly panicked.

What would she do if she failed this test?

How could she afford to keep taking it?

As she looked at all the other questions, she could not remember any of the answers. Looking around the room everyone else seemed to be busy writing. She remembered that her friend has advised her to bring a sweet to suck, and as she unwrapped a mint she took some deep breaths to help calm her rising panic. She looked at the question paper again and noticed there was a picture of the ring road sign which they had been discussing that morning at work. As she read the question she was relieved to find that she not only knew the answer but once again felt confident.

Taking deep breaths can help calm you down when panic sets in.

Rachael forgets her passport

Rachael had put everything she needed for her theory test ready on the table, including her new and unfamiliar red passport which she had only obtained that year. However, when her friend arrived to drive her to the test centre, Rachael quickly grabbed her driving licence and appointment card and dashed out the door. It was only when she arrived at the test centre that she realised that she had left the passport behind.

After a moment's initial panic, she remembered that other proofs of identity were acceptable. The clerk suggested a bus pass or a students union card, but Rachael had neither. She suddenly remembered her Saturday voluntary job at the hospital shop – she had a pass for the Women's Royal Voluntary Services with her photo on. She showed it to the clerk who said it would be acceptable.

> Always check you have everything with you before you set off for the test centre.

William is over confident
William was doing an apprenticeship in a garage so felt very confident as he went into the test centre. He quickly answered all the questions and was out in plenty of time to have coffee with a friend before having to return to work. He was horrified and very embarrassed to discover that he had failed his test and had to resit it. The second time he felt quite nervous, but was determined to read the questions more carefully and spend any time left over re-checking his answers instead of leaving the room and having coffee. His sensible strategy paid off. He passed.

> Always read each question thoroughly before answering. Use any time left over to double check your answers.

DISCUSSION POINTS

1. Do you think that the introduction of the theory test has helped improve the standard of driving generally?

2. Why do you think young drivers are more inclined to be involved in accidents?

3. 'Road rage' is a modern expression: what do you think are the causes of it?

3
Preparing for the Practical Test

ENSURING YOU ARE READY FOR THE PRACTICAL TEST

Before taking your practical driving test you need to have:

- plenty of practice
- confidence in your ability to handle the car in all types of traffic situations.

It is very important that a learner driver does not just learn and practise their driving only on **test routes**. (These are routes which the instructor thinks are likely to be encountered on the actual driving test.)

The wider the variety of roads and traffic conditions you encounter while learning to drive, the more you will feel:

- confident during the test
- able to cope with unexpected hazards
- capable of correcting any minor mistakes you may make.

Remember the criteria of the test are that you:

- drive consistently well and with confidence
- drive without assistance or guidance from anyone
- display consideration and courtesy to other road users at all times.

HAVING THE RIGHT TYPE OF INSTRUCTION

The person who instructs you to drive is perhaps the biggest influence on your:

- attitude to driving
- ability to cope with the unexpected
- understanding and interpretation of *The Highway Code*.

It is therefore very important that your instructor, and any other person you may have practical driving experience with, displays patience and confidence.

A good driver is not always automatically a good instructor, or an ideal person to accompany a learner driver. If the person who sits by your side while you are trying to learn displays nervousness, intolerance or anger, then you are far better finding another instructor: trying to learn with the wrong type of person will not only delay the learning process, but will instil in you the wrong attitude to driving.

Try to have lessons with an approved driving instructor who helps you feel:

- relaxed
- confident
- able to discuss problems.

You may find close members of your family who know you well will shout or belittle your efforts.

If this is the case you are far better not practising with them as these symptoms of panic show that they might be unable to cope if anything went wrong.

Department of Transport Approved Driving Instructors are used to dealing with all types of learners and normally display a high degree of understanding and courtesy.

An approved driving instructor will have an ADI certificate with their photo clearly displayed in the vehicle showing they have studied and been regularly checked on instructional skills.

HAVING A SUITABLE VEHICLE

If the vehicle you intend to take the test in is not insured for a driving test or is not legally roadworthy, then your test will be cancelled and you will lose your money.

Before attending the test ensure your vehicle is:

- insured
- has a current MOT certificate if more than three years old
- has plenty of petrol
- is checked for oil and water
- has clean windows.

As from 4th May 1999 your vehicle must be fitted with

- an interior rear view mirror for use by the examiner
- headrest and seat belts on the passenger's seat.

If you have hired a car to take the test in, check that it is covered by insurance for a learner driver. If you are learning in a driving school car your instructor will ensure all the above are in order.

CHECKING YOUR EYESIGHT IS UP TO STANDARD

Our eyesight is something we take for granted, but it can deteriorate remarkably quickly. Someone whose eyesight was up to the required standard at the beginning of their first driving lesson may find that only a few months later they have difficulty passing the 'eyesight test'.

What the test requires
You should be able to read a vehicle number plate 79.4 mm (3.1 in) high at 20.5 metres (about 67 feet) minimum distance in good daylight.

It is therefore important that you check your eyesight again a couple of weeks before the day of your test in case you need to:

- renew your glasses or
- start wearing glasses.

Lamp posts are normally about 30 metres apart (100 ft). Therefore if you can stand at a lamp post and read a car number parked by the next lamp post then you really have nothing to worry about.

If you cannot read it don't worry. Take five normal paces forward and try again.

If you still cannot read the number plate:

- you could still be within the legal limits
- you should have your eyes professionally checked.

Remember you would automatically fail your driving test if you couldn't read the number plate on the day of your test.

CHECKING THAT YOU HAVE ALL THE CORRECT PAPERWORK

It is a good idea to double-check that all your paperwork is in order at least a week before you take the actual driving test. It is so easy to suddenly find that your road fund licence needed renewing, or your insurance policy has lapsed or even that your provisional licence has been mislaid since you last checked it.

Have you the following certificates and documents to hand?

1. Theory test pass certificate.
2. Provisional licence. This can be either one issued in Great

Britain (GB) or Northern Ireland (NI). If you hold an EU licence and wish to take a test for a category not covered by your full EU licence, you will still need to have a GB provisional licence.

Check you have signed your driving licence.

The car or motorcycle you are driving needs to:

- be legally roadworthy
- have a current MOT certificate if it's over three years old (four years in Northern Ireland)
- show a valid tax disc
- be insured for a learner driver.

The person instructing should have ensured that all these are in order. However, we are all human and far better to ask and check, at least a week before your test, than discover on the actual day that your instructor had been too busy to notice that any of the above was out of date.

CHECKLIST

You should now be confident that:

- you have had the right type of instruction
- you have had plenty of practice over a wide variety of roads
- your vehicle is suitable to take the driving test in
- your eyesight is up to the required standard
- all the paperwork is in order and up to date.

QUESTIONS AND ANSWERS

I have been teaching my wife to drive in a left hand drive car which I bought when we lived in Germany. A friend now tells me that she is not allowed to take her test in it. Is this correct?

It is quite in order to take your driving test in a left hand drive vehicle. However, mirror and all round observation is even more important when you drive such a vehicle, and the examiner will want to see that your wife is aware of this.

My partner says our car has a fully comprehensive insurance cover for any driver. However, when I looked at the policy I could not find any reference to learner drivers. Am I covered?

Even fully comprehensive insurance for any driver does not cover learners unless it so specifies. Contact your insurance company and clarify that you are covered; if in any doubt ask them to give you a signed paper to say that the vehicle is covered for learner drivers.

If I need to cancel my test is it correct that I need to give three working days notice?

No! You now need to give at least **ten** clear working days notice to cancel a test. This does not include weekends, bank holidays or the day of the actual test. You therefore should allow at least two weeks if you wish to cancel a test, otherwise you will forfeit your test fee.

CASE STUDIES

Mary loses her confidence
Mary was in her early 40s when she started learning to drive. She was delighted with her driving instructor, who was very patient, explained everything clearly, and made the lessons interesting. After eight months of lessons Mary was ready for her driving test, but three weeks before the test date her instructor had to cancel all lessons for a week as he was taken ill.

'I'll take you out for some practice,' Mary's husband said. 'It's about time you had practice in our car' and he stuck 'L' plates on the front and rear of the family Rover saloon car.

Mary was not too happy about the idea as the Rover was much larger than the Volkswagen Polo her instructor had been using. When she expressed her reservations her husband was not understanding.

'Don't be stupid,' he said angrily. 'I have paid a fortune for you to learn to drive, you are taking your test in a couple of weeks, and I presume that once you have passed you will be driving our car.'

Mary asked her husband to move the car out from its parking space so she could drive away easily. He refused, remarking that she must know by now how to move off from a parking position.

As Mary sat in the unfamiliar driving seat panic blocked out everything she had been taught. 'Well!' her husband's impatient voice interrupted her thoughts, 'let's get started'.

As Mary tried to remember her cockpit drill, she was painfully aware that every dial, every control was utterly different. 'I can't,' she said, close to tears, 'everything is so different, and I feel frightened.'

The lesson had to be abandoned. Because of her loss of confidence in her ability to drive, Mary's test had to be cancelled. Two years later she tried learning to drive again and eventually passed both her normal driving test and her Advanced Driving Test.

A learner needs to be carefully introduced to a new car. If you are quick tempered or nervous never try to accompany an inexperienced driver; it will not only put a strain on your relationship, but also cause the learner, or even a novice driver, to lose confidence.

Tommy thinks up an excuse

Tommy had already failed two tests, but he had managed to conceal the fact from his mates. The first test he had failed because he had hit the kerb when doing his turn in the road. Embarrassed, he thought it better to tell his mates he had failed for exceeding the speed limit.

On his second test he really did fail for excessive speed, but felt he could hardly tell his friends he had repeated the same fault. All tests after his were cancelled due to fog, so he told his friends his test had been cancelled due to the adverse weather conditions. Now with another test only days away he was trying to think of a suitable excuse in case he failed again. He decided to speak to his instructor about his worries.

The instructor was very surprised that Tommy had such little confidence in his ability to pass. 'You are an excellent driver,' he said. 'However, if you keep thinking you are going to fail your driving test, you will. Think more positively, think how happy you will be when you tell your mates you have passed.'

Have positive thoughts at all times.

William gets a shock

William was feeling very confident as his practical driving test day drew near. Just two days before his test he was having his final lesson when his instructor asked him if there was anything worrying him.

'Not really,' said William. 'We have discussed what happens on the day of the test, and I feel happy about everything.'

'Good,' his instructor replied. 'Remember, the examiner will check your eyesight first, he will ask you to read a number plate, for example, that red car over there.'

William looked at the number plate carefully. 'That's rather a long way away, isn't it? I can barely make out the letters.' His instructor sounded worried as he pointed out another vehicle for William to read the plate. William managed this time, with a little difficulty.

'You had no trouble at that distance when you first started your lessons.' said his instructor. 'I think your eyesight has deteriorated in the last few months'.

William was shocked. He had no idea his eyesight had changed and couldn't bear the thought of failing the test on his eyesight.

'Do you think I should go to one of these instant glasses shops?' he asked.

His instructor thought for a moment. 'You are definitely going to need glasses for driving; however, the distance I am asking you to read a number plate may be slightly in excess of the requirements so you may be all right on your test. However, it's an unnecessary risk, so I suggest you see an optician immediately after this lesson to discuss the matter with him.'

Check your eyesight regularly by reading number plates.

DISCUSSION POINTS

1. Some countries require learner drivers to pass a night test as well as a daytime test. Do you think this is a good idea?

2. Do you think that the theory of driving should be part of the school curriculum?

3. Many people are unaware that their eyesight is failing until it gets quite bad. Do you think it's a good idea that drivers should have an annual eyesight test? Should they carry a certificate to show their eyesight (with glasses if necessary) is up to the required standard?

4
Coping on the Day of
Your Practical Test

HAVING A POSITIVE ATTITUDE

You will pass your practical driving test if you can demonstrate to the examiner that you can drive safely, showing:

- concentration and observation while driving
- consideration and courtesy to all road users
- anticipation
- a sense of responsibility
- patience and confidence.

You will have already taken and passed your theory test and in doing so you will have studied

- the current edition of *The Highway Code*
- the manual *Driving Skills*
- *The Official Theory Test for Cars and Motorcycles.*

This will have given you an excellent background for your practical test. However, this knowledge is only the foundation on which to build your driving skills. Before the day of your practical test you should have:

- practised not only in the area where you intend to take your driving test, but on a wide variety of roads, encountering and coping with as many different hazards as possible
- practised the set exercises so that you feel confident in handling the car in tight situations.

The set exercises
1. Reversing round a corner.
2. Reverse parking.
3. Turning in the road.

These are all very good exercises to demonstrate the correct use of:

- steering
- accelerator
- clutch
- foot brake
- handbrake
- observation.

Adopting a positive attitude

It is very important on the day of your practical test that you feel very positive. If you have doubts about your ability you will demonstrate 'lack of confidence' in your driving; this in turn will tell the examiner that you need more practice before being allowed on the road alone.

Remember you have:

- passed your theory exam, therefore your knowledge of driving theory has been checked
- practised driving on many different roads and encountered many different situations
- proved to your driving instructor that your driving is up to the required standard.

So relax and enjoy demonstrating your driving skills to your examiner.

PRESENTING A GOOD APPEARANCE

First impressions are very important and your examiner, however impartial he may be, is also human, therefore he would feel happier going for a drive with someone who:

- looks clean and tidy
- appears confident and relaxed
- acts politely.

You yourself would feel better and more confident, knowing that you were making a favourable impression.

Make sure your car is also clean and tidy; a dirty car with windows that need a good clean and paper litter all over the floor, is not going to create the impression of a responsible driver.

When you arrive at the test centre

Give your car windows an extra clean before going to meet the examiner. This will:

- give you something positive to do to keep your nerves in check
- demonstrate to the examiner that you are aware of the importance of good all round vision
- improve your vision while driving
- help you to feel more confident.

> Tension breeds tension, so try to feel confident;
> it will help both you and the examiner to relax.

ENSURING YOU HAVE THE NECESSARY PAPERWORK

It's so easy in the general excitement and tension of your driving test day to forget to pick up the most essential things. Make sure you have with you

- your provisional driving licence, which **must be signed**
- the certificate which says you have passed the theory test.

Always double-check you have everything when you get into the car. It has been known for candidates to prepare everything, put it down while they put their coat on, and forget to pick it up again. Also check:

- your car road fund licence has not run out
- your vehicle is insured for you to drive.

ALLOWING TIME FOR PARKING

The area around driving test centres can become very congested on the days when tests are taking place. It can add to your tension if you have difficulty finding a suitable place to park, so on the day of your test you can help yourself feel more relaxed by:

- planning your day carefully, allowing plenty of time not only to drive to the test centre, but also for parking
- checking beforehand if the test centre has toilet facilities. If not, find out where the nearest facilities are.

CHECKLIST

On the day of the test it is important to:

- have a positive attitude
- make an effort to present the correct appearance
- ensure you have the necessary paperwork with you
- allow time for parking.

QUESTIONS AND ANSWERS

I need to pass this test quickly because of my job. Is it true that I must wait a month before I can resit the test if I fail?

You used to have to wait a month. However, you can now resit the test again as soon as you want to. If you do fail it is a good idea to get a little more practice on the points which the examiner brings to your attention, to make sure you don't fail again.

Is it true that examiners have to fail a certain quota of candidates?

No, every candidate is judged on their ability to drive safely. Unfortunately many candidates, through nerves or because they had not had enough practice, fail to show good driving procedures to the examiner, demonstrating that they would not be safe to drive on their own. The examiner has only a short time to make the decision which would allow a person to drive any car on busy roads for the rest of their life.

I always get my rights and lefts mixed up when I am nervous. If I turn the wrong way will I automatically fail my test?

No, the examiner is testing you on your ability to drive safely, however if you turn the wrong way you may end up on a route which is more difficult than he had planned. Driving tests are as uniform as possible and examiners are trained to carry out every test to the same standard. If you turn the wrong way, don't worry, continue driving safely and the examiner will soon get you back on his route.

CASE STUDIES

Molly's friend tries to help her relax
Feeling nervous on the day of her test, Molly decides to go and see

her neighbour for a little moral support. Her neighbour suggested Molly should take two of her tranquillisers.

'They will help you feel nice and relaxed, dear,' she said. 'I use them all the time!'

Molly took the tablets, and she definitely felt relaxed – in fact so relaxed that when she took her test she was doing everything in slow motion, and was a hazard on the road. The test had to be abandoned.

> Never take any form of drug or tranquilliser
> before taking your driving test.

Jane forgets how to start on a hill
On the lesson an hour before her practical test, Jane's instructor stopped her on a hill to practise her hill start.

'I have never pulled out on a hill as steep as this,' said Jane in alarm. 'I don't know what I am supposed to do.'

Jane's instructor knew that not only had Jane practised her hill start here at least four times, but she had also practised on much steeper hills. Her mind had obviously gone blank with nervous tension.

'Now think carefully,' the instructor said kindly. 'How do you normally pull away when you are on an incline?'

'I don't know,' Jane replied, in tears. 'You have never taught me.' Her instructor knew she had been taught well and this sudden loss of memory sometimes happened to people on a driving test.

'Turn the engine off and let us just relax,' said her instructor.

For the next few minutes her instructor discussed various other aspects of driving safely and reading the road, before returning to the problem in hand. 'Do you remember that time we came to those lights on the steep hill, where the car in front started to roll back a little and you did that brilliant hill start?', she reminded Jane.

Jane vaguely remembered, but still had no idea how to do a hill start. Her instructor went over the details about biting point, clutch control, and remembering to make sure you were still at biting point before letting the handbrake off.

Jane tried again and pulled off. Her instructor took her to various other slopes and hills before returning to the original one. Jane did them all perfectly.

'If this happens on your actual test,' the instructor said. 'Take a couple of deep breaths to help you relax.'

Jane completed her test without any problems. She passed.

> Remember to take deep breaths if you find tension
> makes your mind go blank.

John learns a hard lesson

John had been looking forward to his test, he felt confident and had planned to spend the evening before relaxing with a video. About nine o'clock some friends called round and took him out for a drink, to help him feel really relaxed. Unfortunately he had quite a few drinks.

When his instructor called for him next morning, he was alarmed when John stopped at a green traffic light, and further alarmed when John nearly shot a red light. Concerned that John was also driving far too close to the vehicles in front, he asked John to pull in and stop.

'Are you feeling nervous?'

'No,' replied John. 'I feel fine.'

'You haven't been taking any tranquillisers or anything like that?'

'Of course not!' John replied indignantly.

The instructor felt something was wrong as John was an excellent pupil and had been expected to sail through the driving test. He suggested they have a cup of coffee, thinking that perhaps John was feeling nervous and didn't like to admit it.

Over coffee John mentioned how his attempt to watch a video the previous night had been thwarted by his friends. His instructor suddenly became worried and asked him how much he had drunk, and what time he had had his last drink.

'You know why you have been driving so out of character?' he said. 'You are still under the influence of the drink you had last night and early this morning.'

He cancelled John's test. John lost the money he had paid for his test and also learned a valuable lesson – that when you drink the night before, it is still in your system the following morning, affecting your reactions.

> Remember it can take up to twelve hours for alcohol to get
> out of your system. Never drive if you have been drinking,
> it affects your judgement.

DISCUSSION POINTS

1. How many different and sensible ways can you think of to help you feel relaxed?

2. How would you advise a friend who asked you about achieving a smart appearance?

3. What worries you most about the driving test?

5
Meeting Your Examiner

So many stories are told about driving examiners, fuelled no doubt by the fact that normally this is one of the few tests one takes in life where you are alone in a confined space with a complete stranger for over half an hour.

However, if you look at it from the examiner's point of view he too is going to be alone with a complete stranger who thinks he can drive, but is often so nervous he may do irrational things.

It is therefore much easier from both yours and the examiner's point of view if you can relax and think of the examiner as a normal person trying to judge your driving fairly, and without any prejudice.

CONTROLLING YOUR NERVES

You will normally meet your examiner in a room set aside for this. In most test centres there will be more than one examiner, so other people will be waiting for their test.

When the examiner enters the room he will:

- call the name of the candidate he has been asked to examine
- greet you
- check your driving licence
- ask you to sign the form confirming you are the person named on the application form
- expect you to be able to sign a declaration to say your insurance is in order.

For many people even this part of the driving test, simple as it is, causes shaking of the hand while you sign, a feeling of anticipation and nervousness.

If you experience any of these symptoms then:

- take a couple of deep breaths
- think positively (this person is only doing his job)

- remember your instructor says you are ready for this
- suck a sweet.

LEADING THE WAY TO YOUR VEHICLE

The examiner will ask you to 'Lead the way to your vehicle'.
    No doubt he is hopeful that it is a nice clean comfortable car. However, even if you have an old banger it will not make any difference. The examiner is only interested in your ability to be able to drive:

- safely
- considering other road users
- following the rules as laid down in *The Highway Code*.

As you walk to the car the examiner will try to help you relax by talking about the weather or other general items of interest.
    Remember:

- think positive at all times
- look on the examiner as a friend who wants you to pass
- try to enjoy every moment of your test.

After the test everyone will be asking you about it, and it's a shame not to savour every moment. It's a bit like a wedding, most people only hope to do it once, yet the actual ceremony is over too quickly and the people taking part are far too nervous to remember little details.

READING A NUMBER PLATE CORRECTLY

Before you get into your car the examiner will point out a vehicle and ask you to read the number plate. He will say something like this: 'Will you read the number plate of that red car?'
    If you normally wear glasses for driving, then put them on to read the number plate. Don't panic if you have left your glasses in the car:

- explain your glasses are in the car (remember it's quite normal to leave driving glasses in the car)
- fetch them
- treat the examiner as a normal person
- take deep breaths again.

If you can't read the number plate or have difficulty **don't panic**. The examiner will pick another vehicle. Remember the first distance at which he asks you to read a number plate will most likely be well above the required standard.

If you still cannot read the number plate or your answer is incorrect, then the examiner will:

• carefully measure the exact distance
• repeat the test over this distance.

If you still cannot read it then the test will be abandoned and you will have lost your test fee. If you can read it after it has been measured carefully the test will proceed as normal. However, I would strongly advise you to have your eyes tested at the earliest opportunity.

REMEMBERING YOUR FIVE COCKPIT CHECKS

While you are settling into the driving seat, the examiner will be walking around your car to check the number plates, and writing the number down.

Once the examiner is safely in the passenger seat make sure you do your five cockpit checks:

1. Check that all doors are closed properly.
2. Check your seat is in the right position for you:
   – not too close
   – not so far away that you are having to stretch for the foot controls
   and put your seat belt on.
3. Check your mirror is correctly adjusted and that your wing mirrors are still right for you.
4. Check your handbrake is firmly on.
5. Check your gear is in neutral.

If you do these checks carefully it will help you relax and feel less nervous (see Figure 5).

If it will help this is the best time to take out a sweet to suck.

Driving examiners are people too!
Remember driving examiners:

• are carefully trained
• will not try to trick you
• will give clear instruction on where they want you to go

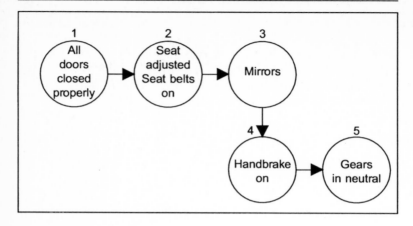

Fig. 5. The five cockpit checks.

- will give more complicated instructions (when they intend to test your emergency stop, manoeuvres *etc*) while you are stationary.
- understand you are feeling apprehensive and nervous (they too have to take regular tests to ensure they are up to standard)
- are normal people trying to do their job.

CHECKLIST

You should now know about:

- controlling your nerves
- meeting your examiner
- leading the way to your vehicle
- checking your eyesight
- running through your five checks.

QUESTIONS AND ANSWERS

I was once attacked by a taxi driver. Ever since I have been terrified to be alone in a car with a man I don't know. I know that the examiners are very carefully selected, but I can't help this awful terror. Can my mother, who has been teaching me, accompany me on my test?

Examiners are quite happy for a candidate's instructor to accompany them on the driving test. However, they must only observe, not take part in any way by offering advice or suggestions.

I have recently been widowed and need to be able to drive as I live in a very isolated place. I did have a driving licence during the 1939/45 war when I was a driver for the Voluntary Aid Detachment. Unfortunately my husband had strong views that a woman's place was in the home, not behind the wheel of a car. I therefore haven't driven since 1948. I am remarkably fit and healthy for my age. Nevertheless, people tell me however well I drive, no examiner will pass me. Is this true?

Every candidate for the driving test is judged solely on their ability to drive safely with due consideration for other road users obeying the rules as set down in *The Highway Code*. Age, sex or race do not enter the equation. I suggest you contact a reputable driving instructor and book a course of lessons. He or she will be in a better position to advise you if and when you are ready for a driving test.

I wear very strong glasses and have been told that before I move off on my driving test, the examiner will ask to see my spare pair. Is this true?

If you wear glasses or contact lenses it is always a good idea to have a spare pair handy in case of mishap. However, the examiner is there solely to test your ability to drive – not to check if you have all the sensible back ups for emergencies.

CASE STUDIES

Andrew starts to panic

Andrew had been learning to drive with his parents and as the date of his practical driving test approached they suggested he should have a couple of lessons with the local driving school.

Andrew felt confident as he met his instructor, and was delighted to see he was going to drive a new Peugeot.

'This is much nicer than my mother's old Fiesta,' he remarked as he got in. His instructor explained the various dials and controls, pointing out that the indicator was not in the same place.

As Andrew went to move off he stalled the car. He suddenly felt stupid and panicky. 'What am I doing?' he thought to himself. 'I haven't done anything like this for ages, and I have to pass this test in ten days – it's so important.'

The instructor tried to get him to relax, but Andrew had become too flustered by the initial stall to think clearly. As he tried to move off again he inadvertently put on the wipers instead of the indicators. He felt such a fool.

The instructor, realising that Andrew was gradually getting into a panic, suggested that they should wait a few minutes for Andrew to calm down.

'I never get nervous or worried like this normally,' said Andrew. 'It's so unlike me.'

His instructor explained that Andrew was so used to driving his mother's car, which no doubt he did very well, that he had made the same movement with the clutch and accelerator as he normally did, forgetting the Peugeot controls were sharper.

The instructor also explained that candidates often over-react on driving tests. 'Candidates make a little mistake, and instead of correcting it and carrying on with their driving, they think they have automatically failed. The big mistake is that candidates tend to dwell on the stupid error they feel they have made, so they don't concentrate on the job in hand, which is driving safely and well.'

Andrew felt that the lesson with a qualified instructor had prepared him for his test in a way he had not foreseen. As he explained to his parents later: 'If anything had gone slightly wrong during my driving test, I would have blown it. Now I realise we all can make small errors, and the secret is to rectify the mistake, without panic, forget about it and carry on planning and looking ahead.'

Andrew passed his test two weeks later.

> When driving you must always concentrate and look ahead. If you dwell on what has happened, instead of planning and looking ahead, you could cause an accident.

Mrs Pilkington-Brown finds examiners are not so frightening

Mrs Pilkington-Brown had not been an easy person to teach to drive. Her husband had refused to accompany her on practice lessons after an initial disastrous outing. She had worked her way through most of the driving schools in the area, ending up with a small school with a lady instructor. By the time Mrs Pilkington-Brown was ready for a test, she had lost count of the number of tuition hours she had received.

On the day of the test her instructor called for her in good time, so there could be a last minute practice.

'I've decided I am not going to take my test,' Mrs Pilkington-Brown said firmly.

'But you have worked so hard for this day,' her instructor said in dismay, thinking how hard they had both worked to get Mrs Pilkington-Brown to this stage.

'No! I am not going to take this test, and nothing you say will change my mind,' was the firm reply. 'Well, I feel you should explain this yourself to the driving examiner,' her instructor replied. 'It would be most rude not to turn up. Also as you have paid for this lesson you might as well drive there.'

Mrs Pilkington-Brown eventually agreed after a little persuasion, reiterating that she was definitely not going to take the test.

On arrival at the test centre three other candidates with their instructors were waiting apprehensively for the examiners. When one examiner called out Mrs Pilkington-Brown's name her instructor started to explain that Mrs Pilkington-Brown was feeling far too nervous to sit her test.

The examiner sat down beside Mrs Pilkington-Brown and said in a friendly relaxing voice, 'Surely you are not going to worry about going out for a drive with me on such a lovely day?' For a moment there was silence as the examiner smiled at the tired, angry looking woman by his side. A rare smile appeared on Mrs Pilkington-Brown's face. She turned to her instructor and said, 'You don't have to worry about me any more, Mrs Johnson. I will be quite all right with this gentleman.'

Without another look at her instructor she led the way to her vehicle. She passed her test.

Examiners are not ogres. They understand how nervous candidates can be when taking a driving test.

Adrian overcomes his nerves

Adrian was surprised how nervous he felt as he walked with the examiner towards his car, although the examiner seemed very pleasant and remarked about the changeable weather they had been having.

Before reaching Adrian's car, the examiner stopped to ask him to read a number plate. Adrian's voice sounded really croaky as he nervously read the required number plate.

'Why am I feeling so worried and nervous about this driving test?' Adrian wondered. 'My mouth feels dry, I feel I am going to mess the whole thing up. This is so unlike me.'

As Adrian got into the car he took a couple of deep breaths, remembering that he had been told this helped to relax you. As he started to check his doors, seat and mirrors, he spotted the mints he had bought on his instructor's advice that 'sucking a sweet could help if you started to feel nervous'. Perhaps it would also help get rid of the dry feeling in his throat.

As he unwrapped the sweet, he offered one to the examiner, who said as he declined the offer, 'Had to give them up, I was addicted to them and my dentist advised me against eating so many sweets.'

Sucking the mint, Adrian carried on with his basic cockpit checks. Handbrake on, gear in neutral. As he turned to the examiner, he noted he was smiling. Adrian could feel the nervous tension gradually draining away.

'Why was I so worked up about this test?' he thought. 'I am going to drive well and pass this test.'

> When you start feeling nervous take a couple of deep breaths and it's also a good idea to suck a sweet.

DISCUSSION POINTS

1. How would you advise someone who was going for an exam or a job interview to overcome their feeling of nervousness?

2. In some countries the candidate on a driving test is accompanied by his instructor throughout the whole test. Do you think this practice should be adopted in this country?

3. How would you relax a person who was feeling nervous with you?

6
Moving Off Smoothly

STARTING THE ENGINE

Once you have done your cockpit checks the examiner will ask you to 'Follow the road ahead'.

He will explain that he will ask you in plenty of time when he wants you to turn left or right. Before you start the engine get into the habit of always re-checking that:

- your handbrake is firmly on
- your gear lever is in neutral.

So although you have just done your basic cockpit checks, check again the handbrake and gear lever before starting the engine.

Sometimes people feel so nervous and apprehensive at this stage they experience difficulties in inserting and turning the key. If this happens to you: don't worry and take deep breaths.

The examiner will understand how you feel and often it helps if you say something like 'I am feeling a bit nervous today'. The examiner is human and he knows if you are relaxed you will drive:

- more safely
- more observantly
- with better concentration on your driving

so he will most likely advise you to 'take your time'.

MOVING AWAY FROM THE KERB

Throughout your test and during your driving life, **moving off smoothly and safely** is perhaps one of the most important aspects. Never move off before you have checked properly that it is safe to do so by:

- using your mirrors
- checking your blind spot by looking over your shoulder.

Most people feel nervous on the initial pull away from the kerb. If you do, remember: **deep breaths can help** you to:

- clear your head
- concentrate on the job in hand.

There may be other people on their driving test who are pulling away from the kerb at the same time. They too will probably be feeling nervous, therefore your initial pull out,requires greater:

- observation
- concentration
- awareness of dangers from blind spot areas.

Be particularly aware of any pedestrians who may be crossing the road in the area.

BALANCING YOUR CLUTCH AND ACCELERATOR

The correct balance of your clutch and accelerator is the key to moving off smoothly and safely, without kangarooing or stalling (see Figure 6).

You will have practised this hundreds of times while learning to drive so it's very frustrating and upsetting if you find yourself doing it badly on your test.

If you start to kangaroo
- think of that Rolf Harris song 'Tie my Kangaroo *down*'
- push your clutch down.

Never try to rush this part of your test – a smooth start will boost your confidence.

If you make mistakes remember to take a couple of deep breaths. The examiner understands your feelings; he has tested dozens of people, and it's very rare that a candidate does not display some form of nervousness.

If you stall
- put your handbrake on
- put your gear lever back to neutral position
- start the engine again
- proceed with the normal pull out drill.

Always remember even the most experienced drivers sometimes stall the car. I always think it's a bit like sneezing: you don't want to do it, but it sometimes happens.

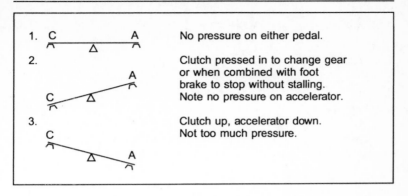

Fig. 6. The see-saw movement of clutch and accelerator.

If you stall again
- put your handbrake on
- put your gear level in neutral
- check your seat is positioned correctly for you.

It's very easy when you are feeling nervous to want to sit too close to the wheel.

Always remember
Badly adjusted seating can cause drivers to stall or over accelerate, therefore your seat position could make all the difference to how you drive.

Never forget to check your **mirror** after you have altered your seating position.

CHECKLIST

You should now feel confident about:

- knowing what to do if you start feeling nervous
- coping with a stall
- regaining control if you start to kangaroo
- balancing your clutch and accelerator correctly
- adjusting your seat again if necessary.

QUESTIONS AND ANSWERS

I am worried that while I am meeting the examiner and away from the car, another vehicle might park so close that I would have difficulty moving my car away from the kerb. I feel quite confident about the test, but having to cope with extra manoeuvring at this early stage would be quite stressful. What would happen in a situation like this?

If anything like this happened, which would be very unusual, the examiner would have no objection to your instructor, who accompanied you to the test centre, moving the car to a more suitable position. Examiners want you to feel as relaxed as possible when you start the driving test, therefore they always give you a straightforward drive to start with.

I have been advised to adjust my inside mirror so that I have to move my head every time I use the mirror so that the examiner sees I am checking it correctly. Is this a good idea?

Always have your mirror correctly adjusted so that you can observe quickly and easily what is happening behind you. You should be checking the mirror not only when you are going to indicate or change direction, but often enough to always be aware what is behind you and of any dangers from that direction. Mirrors should be adjusted so that a slight movement of the eyes is all that is necessary, this should only take a split second. Examiners are well trained and know if you are using the mirror correctly; having it incorrectly adjusted not only will cause neck strain, with constant turning of your head, but could prove potentially dangerous.

Is it always necessary to indicate when you move away from the kerb?

You indicate to make other road users aware of your intentions. This includes not only vehicles, but cyclists and pedestrians as well. It is therefore very important you really look around before you move away from the kerb; if there are other stationary cars around you should indicate as they may be hiding other road users in your blind spot. However, if there are no vehicles or people around, then it is quite in order not to indicate. It is worth remembering that in some countries you have to indicate, by law, every time you move away from the kerb or change direction. Personally I always indicate for my initial pull away from the kerb.

CASE STUDIES

Kathleen has a giggle

Kathleen was feeling very nervous as she carefully did her cockpit checks. She was painfully aware that the examiner was watching her every move.

As she slipped the gear into first, and checked her shoulder and mirror, she tried hard to forget this stranger sitting next to her. As she increased her pressure on the accelerator, and gently lifted her clutch she gave a final mirror check, intending to move away smoothly and safely.

Nothing happened.

For a moment Kathleen couldn't understand what had happened, then she realised she had forgotten to switch the engine on.

'It might be a good idea to start the engine,' she spoke without thinking. 'Cars with engines always go better,' she added with a nervous giggle. Then realising she was on her test, she turned to look at the examiner. He was smiling broadly.

Suddenly Kathleen relaxed – this man was human, why had she got herself in such a nervous state? She checked her handbrake was on, gear in neutral and started the engine. As she pulled safely away from the kerb she couldn't resist saying out loud, 'I think that was a little better.'

If things don't go according to plan, don't panic.

Robin forgets the key

Robin's driving test had been cancelled twice because of bad weather, so he felt quite excited, yet confident, as he at last sat in the car with the examiner. After the explanation about following the road ahead, and that if any instructions were not understood just say and they would be repeated, Robin went to start the engine and was horrified to find he did not have the key.

'The key' he exclaimed in horror. 'My father forgot to give it to me.'

'Look,' the examiner said kindly, 'is that your father standing at the end of the road watching us?'

He had hardly got the words out before Robin was sprinting towards the corner. When he returned, the key safe in his hand, looking very flustered, the examiner said: 'I think that is the second time that has happened this month. Because we have no test centre in this area and meet our candidates in the street, we often find if they have been driven here that the instructor either leaves the key in the ignition while we do the eyesight test, or forgets to hand the key over.'

Robin took a couple of deep breaths to relax himself again, glad that the examiner understood.

> Always make sure you have the ignition key with you.

Mrs Jones kangaroos

Mrs Jones was apprehensive about her test. She knew she was rather elderly to be taking a test for the first time. However, since her husband Bob had had his stroke, they had been so cut off without the car. She had had to learn. It had been hard work, cost a lot in lessons, but both she and her instructor were confident she would pass. The only problem was the blue Metro she had learned in had broken down yesterday, and she was not too happy about this red one. Her instructor had said it was a much better and newer car, it was only four weeks old. However, she had had problems driving to the test centre. The clutch felt so different from 'Baby Blue', as she had affectionately called the other car.

As she sat in the car, checking her controls carefully, she said a little prayer. This test was so important.

As she moved off the car started to 'kangaroo'; remembering what her instructor had told her she carefully pushed the clutch in a little, only to repeat the kangaroo as she lifted it again. It was all too much. She stopped the car, turned off the engine, and turning to her examiner she said, 'It's no good, this car may be new, but it feels so different from Baby Blue, that's the car I usually drive.' She could feel the tears welling up.

'I see you have some mints there,' the examiner said kindly. 'Why not have one of those and start again?' As Mrs Jones reached for the mints which her instructor had thoughtfully left, the examiner added, 'Everyone feels strange at first in a car they are not used to driving. Just take your time and when you are ready we will start again.'

Mrs Jones relaxed and went on to pass her test.

> Try not to take your test in an unfamiliar car. If you have to, make sure you have had at least an hours' tuition in it, particularly on stops and starts and manoeuvring.

DISCUSSION POINTS

1. How do you relax when you feel nervous?

2. Should a driving test be longer than it is?

3. In many countries the minimum age for driving is higher than in the UK. Do you think we should raise the minimum age?

7
Reading the Road Ahead

UNDERSTANDING THE IMPORTANCE OF FORWARD PLANNING

After the initial hurdles of meeting your examiner and the eyesight test, you should be feeling a little more relaxed. It is very important that you don't have any negative or irrelevant thoughts – while driving you must at all times:

- think ahead
- plan ahead
- look ahead.

Forget about the examiner sitting beside you. Throughout your driving life you will have all kinds of people in the passenger seat, some you will like and some you won't. You may have to drive when people in your vehicle have been drinking and are aggressive, excited and noisy.

You will most likely at some time in your driving life have children in the car who may be:

- crying
- quarrelling
- asking questions.

You will also have to drive at times when you are feeling unhappy, depressed or worried and at times of great stress such as after receiving bad news, and when you are excited or happy.

Whatever is happening in the car, or what your personal thoughts are, the safety of yourself and other road users depends on you not only looking and planning ahead at all times, but also being aware of what is happening on all four sides of your car. If you make an error:

- correct it
- forget it
- get on with the job in hand, which is driving safely.

When taking a driving test, it is easy to be too self critical. Many people fail their driving test because they make a small error, for example stalling. Many learners find that if they stall during a test, especially if they do so more than once, they keep thinking about it and make more mistakes because they are unable to concentrate, which in turn affects their ability to anticipate.

ACTING ON SIGNS AND SIGNALS

You will be expected to obey all traffic signs, also to act upon markings painted on the road. Signs are an essential part of any road or traffic system; they are there not to decorate the road and give employment to people, but to:

- warn
- inform.

It is therefore very important that you:

- observe all signs
- act on what they tell you.

Memorise the sequence of traffic lights (see Figure 7) so you know what to expect when approaching lights that are changing.

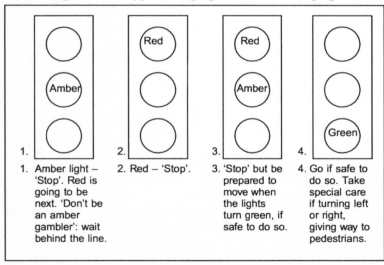

1. Amber light – 'Stop'. Red is going to be next. 'Don't be an amber gambler': wait behind the line.

2. Red – 'Stop'.

3. 'Stop' but be prepared to move when the lights turn green, if safe to do so.

4. Go if safe to do so. Take special care if turning left or right, giving way to pedestrians.

Fig. 7. Understanding the sequence of traffic lights.

Approaching a stop sign

When approaching a stop sign, there is normally no need to come down to second gear. You are going to have to stop at this type of junction in any case, so avoid unnecessary changing of gears. **Remember to STOP at the stop line.**

It's so easy to just pause and look, not really stop. Therefore to ensure you have stopped completely, **apply your handbrake once the car is stationary**.

Although in normal driving you would not always need to apply the handbrake once you have stopped, on your test it is advisable to do so, as sometimes candidates do not stop completely and thus fail their test.

Usually junctions which have a stop line are:

- more dangerous to pull out from
- require more observation
- have a blind spot.

Remember:

- If, when you have stopped, you find your vision is obstructed by a vehicle, a tree, or maybe a bend in the road, you can then creep forward a little to obtain a better vision. However, always stop fully first at the stop lines.

Approaching a 'give way' sign

When approaching a 'give way' junction:

- look and plan well ahead
- make sure you are in the correct gear to pull out immediately if the road is clear.

You don't have to stop at 'give way' lines; however, if you do there should be no need to apply the handbrake unless you have to wait for more than a few seconds. Unnecessary use of the handbrake at 'give way' lines could impede the flow of traffic.

Ignore illegal signals
Be very careful if another driver waves you on – remember he may be willing to wait, but other vehicles may not be aware of what he is doing and could:

- overtake
- pass on the inside.

There may also be:

- pedestrians
- cyclists
- motorcyclists

which the other driver has not noticed.

- Never give illegal signs (wave someone to come on).
- Never obey illegal signals (signals given by other motorists).

Remember the rules:

1. Signals are to let others, including pedestrians, know what you intend to do.

2. Signals are to help other road users: you know what you intend to do, so inform others.

3. Signals should be given in plenty of time: let people know you intend to pull out or turn right, not 'I am now turning right' or 'I am pulling out' as you actually do it.

4. Signals used must only be the ones laid down in *The Highway Code*: illegal signals confuse and can cause accidents.

BEING IN THE RIGHT GEAR AT THE RIGHT TIME

Your examiner will want to see that you can use all the controls:

- smoothly
- correctly
- at the right time

having full control of your vehicle the whole time.

If you are nervous, which is quite natural, you may drive a little less smoothly than normal at first. However, you should find after a short while you will relax, start to concentrate on your driving, and drive well.

Remember if you feel you are getting too nervous take deep breaths. Breathing in oxygen helps clear your head, enabling you to think clearly.

Using the gears

While you are driving you should always be:

- in the right gear at the right time
- in the right position in the road.

Use your gears wisely and remember:

- approaching a 'stop' line you can stop in third gear
- approaching 'give way' junctions it is normally best to change to second gear, as it gives you the extra acceleration needed to carry on if the road is clear
- keep up with the traffic flow when it is safe and correct to do so.

These practices show confidence and also reduce frustration for following drivers. Remember particularly at junctions:

- be alert
- ensure you are in the correct gear.

Do not be too hesitant at junctions: this can display a lack of confidence and traffic judgement. Be prepared to proceed as soon as it is safe to do so.

OBSERVING WHAT IS HAPPENING ALL AROUND YOU

While driving it is very important that you are:

- looking well ahead at all times
- aware of what is happening behind you
- aware of what is happening on either side of you.

By knowing exactly what is happening on all four sides of your car, it is easier to:

- plan well ahead
- anticipate any dangers well in advance
- adjust your speed to suit the road and traffic conditions.

It is very important while driving along that you:

- leave a safe distance between other vehicles and yourself
- show awareness of cyclists or motorcyclists who may be on your inside.

Never stop too close behind a vehicle. You should be able to see the bottom of the rear tyres in front of you when you are stopped.

Never just follow the car in front; look well beyond so you can anticipate in plenty of time the actions of other vehicles.

CHECKLIST

You should now understand the importance of:

- forward planing as you are driving
- using your handbrake at 'stop' lines
- minimising hesitation at road junctions
- being in the right gear at the right time
- breathing deeply to help clear nervous tension
- observation.

QUESTIONS AND ANSWERS

Cyclists always worry me! If I want to turn left and a cyclist is between me and the left turn should I accelerate a little to get by before I turn, or just slow right down and keep behind him? If I do the latter won't I cause traffic behind to be held up. What do you advise?

This is a problem which affects not only people learning to drive, but also some experienced drivers. Your first consideration is the cyclist:

- You must not cause him to brake.
- You must remember he is also moving at a steady speed, and if he is not turning he will continue at that speed.

You, however, are going to have to slow down to turn into the new road. So unless you are a considerable distance from the junction you wish to turn into, keep well behind the cyclist. Indicate that you intend to turn left: this informs following traffic why you have slowed down.

If I am on my test and a sign indicating there are 'men at work' is followed by a sign restricting traffic to 10 mph, do I need to drop to this very slow speed if other traffic is not doing so, and there are no men working there at that time?

The examiner expects you to obey all road signs and if you see such a sign restricting your speed, you must obey it. However, once you have passed the obvious hazard, usually road works, then you can return to your normal speed.

I have a problem which causes me to make frequent visits to the toilet. What should I do if I need to go to the toilet on my test?

The actual driving test only takes 40 minutes from the time the examiner greets you to the time he leaves your car. It is always advisable to go to the toilet just before you meet your examiner. The majority of test centres have some facilities; if not a notice will explain where the nearest toilet facilities are. Usually once you are driving you are concentrating so hard that you forget the worry of this. However, if your problem is serious and you are unable to wait 40 minutes this should be declared on your application form, or you could speak to your doctor.

CASE STUDIES

David forgets a golden rule

David had found it fairly easy to learn to drive. Both he and his instructor were confident that he would have no problems passing his test. During his test he was asked to turn right on a fairly busy road. As David waited at the junction for the oncoming traffic to pass, the driver of a slow-moving double decker bus flashed his lights and waved his hand indicating to David that he could turn in front of the bus.

As David turned, a motorcyclist came out from the near side of the bus, causing David to stop suddenly, and the motorcyclist to swerve into the kerb, where he fell off.

David was appalled that he had forgotten the danger of illegal signals. Fortunately the motorcyclist was not hurt, but David had learned a valuable lesson.

> Never give illegal signals. Remember, if someone signals you to go, he is speaking for himself, not the rest of the road users in the area.

Eileen is not observant

Eileen had already failed her test twice, each time on a silly thing. She knew she could handle the car well, but each time she took her test something unusual happened. On the first test she had continued to reverse as a man riding a horse had come up behind her.

'If it had been a car,' she explained to her driving instructor later, 'I would have stopped, but somehow a horse did not register as a road user.'

On her second test a young man had run from a side road right onto a pedestrian crossing, causing the examiner to take action. Eileen had not reacted quickly enough. Now on her third test she was concentrating very hard on all that was happening on all sides of the car. The delivery van in front of her had put on his left indicator and stopped. Eileen waited patiently thinking to herself that the driver was waiting a long time to turn left, so she was a little surprised when the examiner suddenly spoke.

'I'm sorry,' he said politely. 'Did you not notice the driver had got out of that vehicle in front of us? I think we could be waiting here a long time.'

Eileen failed her test on her lack of observation.

> Always observe what is happening. Delivery vehicles often stop in non-stopping areas to deliver a parcel or to ask the way.

Mr Henderson follows the bus

Mr Henderson, chief librarian at the local library, was a very precise person who always obeyed the rules. He was feeling confident on his test and found the examiner pleasant and his instructions clear.

'Would you take the next available turn on the left please?' requested his examiner.

Mr Henderson kept well back from the bus in front, which also appeared to be going left, or maybe stopping at a stop.

'Ah,' thought Mr Henderson as he noticed the bus was turning into a side road, 'he is going the same way as me.' As he followed the bus round the corner, he realised he was entering a road reserved for buses only. He had been so busy watching the bus he had failed to observe the relevant road sign.

> Always observe and obey road signs.

DISCUSSION POINTS

1. Everyone has weaknesses in their driving. What are yours?

2. What are the main dangers to be aware of when turning right?

3. Do you think loud radios in a car are a distraction to other drivers? Give reasons for your answer.

8
Doing the Manoeuvres Correctly

The manoeuvres are what candidates worry about perhaps more than any other part of the test. Yet this is the part of the test when you can quietly demonstrate your skills in:

- observation
- consideration for other road users
- control of your vehicle.

Always remember you should never try to do the manoeuvres too fast, which could be very dangerous, especially when moving backwards. You should also try to keep the engine running smoothly without undue noisy acceleration.

The three special manoeuvres you could be asked to do are:

- **reversing** around a corner
- **reverse parking** behind a car or reverse parking into a bay
- **turning in the road**.

The reversing exercises may be carried out in the area of the test centre before or after the test.

UNDERSTANDING THE IMPORTANCE OF CLUTCH CONTROL

On all three manoeuvres the secret is to be able to move your vehicle smoothly and slowly, while being aware at all times what is happening on all sides of your vehicle. To be able to do this successfully you need to control your clutch, so the vehicle moves at the speed you want it to.

Remember:

- to move slower – push your clutch in a little
- to move a little faster – lift your clutch up a little.

Controlling the vehicle with the clutch gives you plenty of time to:

- observe where you are going

- check there are no elderly people, children or dogs in the area who have not noticed you are manoeuvring your vehicle.
- slow down and stop smoothly if another vehicle approaches.

The examiner will not expect you to rush any of the manoeuvres. To do so could be dangerous and would not allow the necessary observation which is one of the important aspects which the examiner will be checking for. However, he will expect you to move the car:

- steadily – no excessive roaring of the engine
- safely – demonstrating awareness of any potential danger.

BEING EXTRA OBSERVANT AT ALL TIMES

During your normal driving you should always be alert for any hazard, and observant of all signs and changing traffic conditions. On your manoeuvres extra observation is called for. Why? you may ask, after all you no doubt feel you are observant enough when you drive normally. The reasons for extra care and attention on any of the manoeuvres are:

1. People, especially pedestrians and children, expect a car to move forward, therefore they are likely to walk behind a car. You must be aware of this whenever you are travelling backwards, and keep checking behind your vehicle.

2. Cyclists may try passing either side of you while you are doing a turn in the road, so keep looking from side to side.

3. Both on the reverse park and reversing around a corner, the front of your car will swing out as you pull your wheel to the left. If any vehicle is in the vicinity you need to be aware of this and stop if necessary.

It is not good enough to just look in your mirrors when manoeuvring – you need to turn your body and really check all round you.

KNOWING WHAT TO DO IF YOUR MANOEUVRING IS GOING WRONG

Reversing
When you are on the test it is easy to panic when things start to go wrong. The manoeuvres are the easiest things to correct. If, for

example you start to reverse and feel you have started off too near the kerb:

- Stop. Go forward a few metres, pulling away from the kerb a little, and start again.

If on your reverse you become muddled about which way to turn the wheel, remember the 'golden rule':

- Driving backwards you turn the wheel the way you want the back of the car to go. Therefore if you want the back to go nearer the kerb, you pull the steering wheel towards the kerb. If you feel you are getting too close to the kerb, turn the wheel away from the kerb.

Remember:

- If the wheels on your car are not straight you might have to give a couple of good pulls.
- Never just look at the back of the car when reversing, look well down the road – just as when driving forward you never look at the front of the bonnet, you look where you want to be not where you are now.

If a car comes up behind you in the side road you are about to reverse into:

- Stop. Move forward into the road you have just come from, wait for the car to go and re-start your manoeuvre.

If you have entered the side road and realise you are too near the kerb and if you move back any more would probably mount it:

- Stop. Move forward a couple of metres, then continue with your reverse, remembering to look well behind you so you can steer a steady course.

Turning in the road

If on the turn in the road you have moved forward, stopped, prepared to move backwards and find yourself moving forward towards the kerb:

- Stop. Check you are in reverse gear. Remember there's a slope down to the kerb, so you need to get your bite on the clutch before releasing the handbrake.

If, on a turn in the road you mess it up and are not going to do it in three manoeuvres:

- Don't worry, go backwards and forwards again using the clutch to go slowly, remembering your observation.

Reverse parking

If, on your reverse park, someone drives into the place you were going to reverse into:

- The examiner will ask you to continue driving ahead. He will suggest another suitable place for you to carry out the manoeuvre.

If you stall the car in the middle of your manoeuvres:

- Don't worry, we all stall the car sometimes. Apply the handbrake, check your gear is in neutral. Start the engine again, then carry on as normal.

UNDERSTANDING THE IMPORTANCE OF POSITIVE THINKING

At all times during your driving test you must:

- think positively
- think logically
- use your common sense.

Examples

If you felt you were messing up your reverse and were likely to mount or hit the kerb, surely it would be sensible and logical to stop and move forward a little.

If you were reversing into your garage at home and thought you were in a bad position and likely to scrape the car on the wall what would you most likely do? You could:

a.   ask someone else to reverse the car into the garage for you
b.   leave the car parked outside the garage
c.   drive forward a little and start again.

If you knew you were going to hit the side of the garage, damaging both the garage and the car, how would you explain to your family and friends that you had started to travel in reverse so had to carry on? They would think you were mad and definitely not fit to be in charge of a car.

The most logical thing to do in this kind of circumstance is to drive forward a little and start again.

Never think 'I'm going to make a mess of this, I'm going to fail this test'; instead think, 'What is the safest and best thing to do in this situation?'

> Remember: When reversing look well back to where
> you want to be.

Always when you are driving be prepared for the unexpected:

- look well ahead
- know what is happening all around you
- use your mirrors wisely
- show consideration for other road users.

Never presume you have failed at any point during the test. The examiner is paid to examine you, he will decide if a certain action by you was potentially dangerous or not.

Just because the examiner is writing something down, don't jump to the conclusion it is negative. Concentrate on your driving and let the examiner get on with his job, he has a lot of paperwork to do.

Never have doubts about your ability to cope with the situation in hand. You have worked hard at learning to drive and your instructor would not have entered you for your test unless he thought you were ready to drive alone and make the right decisions.

CHECKLIST

You should be aware of:

- importance of clutch control, particularly during your manoeuvres
- observation at all times on all sides of your vehicle
- decisions you can make when things appear to be going wrong
- thinking positively.

QUESTIONS AND ANSWERS

I always seem to be miles from the kerb when I am reversing round a corner, particularly when I am halfway round it. How can I avoid getting into this situation?

A car does not bend in the middle, so when you actually turn the corner, the front is following the car and will swing out into the road. This gives the impression that you are a long way from the kerb at that point. Once you are around the corner look well back down the road you are entering. Steer gently, moving nearer the kerb if necessary, remembering to turn the wheel the way you want the back of the car to travel.

I have heard people say you need to 'feather' the wheel at the end of a reverse. What does this mean?

When you have reversed around the corner, you sometimes find although the car appears to be straight, as soon as you move back a little more without moving your steering wheel, the vehicle starts to veer to the left or right. This happens when you have turned the wheel sharply, and although the car looks as though it is in a straight position, the front wheels are still turned to the left or right. You therefore need to 'feather' the steering wheel by pulling it a little to the right, and then perhaps a little to the left, until you reach the position where not only the car is straight, but the wheels are straight, enabling you to travel backwards in a relatively straight line, holding the steering wheel still.

There are several trees in the area where they normally do the 'turn in the roads' on the driving test. I am worried that I will hit the trees when reversing, as they are right on the edge of the pavement. How can I avoid this?

Trees can cut your turning areas by a quarter if you start your turn with a tree directly in front of you. The secret is to start the manoeuvre from a position *beside* a tree. This will ensure that that particular tree will not interfere with your manoeuvre in any way.

If you think logically about it, as you move forward pulling your steering wheel to the right, you will be pulling away from the tree. On your reverse part of the manoeuvre you will most likely find that you are reversing into a clear area between trees (see Figure 8).

The same rule applies to lamp posts. Stop beside one, never have one in front of you when you start to do a 'turn in the road'. However, do check that it hasn't a bus stop sign attached to it.

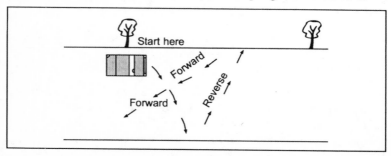

Fig. 8. Turning in a road lined with trees.

CASE STUDIES

Jean remembers to be positive

Jean could feel herself getting more nervous as her test progressed. To pass was vitally important to her as she was due to start a new job and had to produce a full driving licence before she was issued with the car that went with the job.

Jean had felt confident that she would pass the test easily, and was taken aback by how nervous and negative she felt. She kept thinking what would she do if she failed. 'Pull yourself together,' she said to herself as she stalled for the third time.

Later, when the examiner asked her to pull in and stop, then asked her to park behind the red car in front, Jean suddenly remembered her instructor's words about thinking positively. 'Well,' she thought to herself, 'I should be pretty good at this, after all where I live I always have to park in a really narrow area after my lessons, and I can show the examiner how observant I am.'

She smiled to herself, remembering that even her children had had to learn the importance of observation, as living on a busy road even opening a car door required caution. As she started to do the reverse park she found she was starting to relax a little. She suddenly felt very much in control of the situation, and started to enjoy the rest of her test. She was therefore amazed to find she was back outside the test centre. Surely she hadn't been out long enough. However, she was delighted to hear she had passed. The examiner remarked that she had seemed very nervous and hesitant initially, but had suddenly relaxed and handled the car very well.

> Think positively at all times.

William gets a fright

William thought he was doing quite well on his driving test. Everything seemed to be going according to plan. When the examiner asked him to do a reverse park, he remembered to have a good look around and check that it was safe to go backwards before he moved the car. He had just started to turn the wheel to the left, so the rear of the car could enter the parking place, when he was startled by a loud blast of a horn. He stopped immediately, and in front of him saw a furniture van with an angry, gesticulating driver.

William realised he had been so busy concentrating on his reverse park that, although the road had been clear at the start of the manoeuvre, he had forgotten to check to the front again before turning the wheel to go into the area where he wanted to park. The result was his front had moved into the path of oncoming traffic, causing the van to come to an abrupt stop.

> When driving backwards, always double check for
> oncoming vehicles before you start to turn the wheel,
> as your front will swing into any oncoming traffic.
> Observation is vitally important.

John uses his common sense

John had been asked to do a reverse around a corner on his test. At first he felt quite happy; however, after having to stop twice because of cars coming up behind him, John tried to hurry things up a little. As he went to straighten up at the end of the reverse, he realised he was too close to the kerb and, if he carried on, would most likely nudge it. He stopped, thought for a second, then moved forward a little so he was not so near the kerb. Putting the gear back into reverse he carried on backwards to complete his reverse.

> Manoeuvres often call for common sense.

DISCUSSION POINTS

1. All manoeuvres are expected to be carried out with maximum observation. Can you list six reasons why?

2. Parking behind a vehicle calls for extra skills: can you think what they are?

3. In a normal car park would you reverse into your parking slot, or go in forward? What are the advantages and disadvantages of both approaches?

9
Understanding the
Examiner's Requests

When you are feeling apprehensive or nervous, it is easy to misunderstand what is being said to you. Under stress normal conversation can sometimes become confusing, even terrifying: it is for this reason that all examiners have to learn standard expressions when training for their job. Originally the expressions were very rigid and spoken in a much more clockwork manner than nowadays.

Today you will find the examiner much more approachable. However, he has an important job to do which requires a lot of concentration. Remember that you too need to concentrate on your driving.

Putting you at your ease
Contrary to all rumours and tall stories, examiners do try to put the candidate at ease without being too familiar.

The initial requests to:

- see your provisional licence
- lead the way to your vehicle
- read the number plate

are straightforward requests and easy to understand.

FOLLOWING THE ROAD AHEAD

Once you are seated in the car, and have done your five basic checks:

- doors all closed properly
- seat adjusted correctly and your seat belt on
- mirrors adjusted properly
- handbrake firmly on
- gear lever in neutral

the examiner will use an expression similar to this:

'Follow the road ahead unless the traffic signs direct you otherwise or unless I ask you to turn, which I'll do in good time. Move off when you are ready, please.'

Because so many people are nervous or apprehensive they often misunderstand this simple request. All the examiner wants you to do is to:

- drive normally
- look out for traffic signs
- obey them.

As you drive you need to look well ahead, particularly observing all the 'stop' or 'give way' signs. Unless there is a sign directing all traffic to turn or the examiner requests otherwise, go straight ahead at any junction.

It's a bit like being directed somewhere by a non-driver. You have no idea where you are going, you simply follow their directions. However, you as a driver have to be aware of all the road signs, road markings and traffic conditions, to be able to drive them safely to their destination.

When the examiner wants you to turn left, for example, he will say, 'Take the next available road on the left, please.'

Remember you are a driver so observe at all times what type of road you are entering. Be particularly careful not to enter a road that has 'no entry' on it.

If you are in any doubt what the examiner means ask him to repeat his request.

Don't worry if you turn right instead of left. The examiner is there to check that you are safe to drive alone, not that you can follow his instructions. As long as you gave the correct signals and did the turn safely, and you have not entered a restricted area, there will be no problem. The examiner will just direct you back onto the route he wanted you to take. However, it does help if you go the way he wants you to, as otherwise you may end up driving along a far more difficult route than he intended you to.

If you normally have difficulty remembering your 'right' and 'left' when you are feeling nervous or apprehensive, you are in good company, as many people on a driving lesson or test worry about turning the wrong way because they mix up their rights and lefts. To help you remember you can do one of the following:

- Write a big 'R' and 'L' with felt tip on the back of each hand.
- Wear a ring on one of your fingers on the right hand, to remind you that that is the 'R' for ring and right.

You could also remember that:

- you are sitting on the 'right', and hope you are doing everything right
- the examiner is sitting on the 'left' and you hope he can be left behind in the future.

SELECTING A SAFE PLACE TO STOP

Throughout the test the examiner will ask you to pull up and stop many times. The expression he will probably use is 'Pull up on the left at a convenient place, please'.

The key word here is **convenient**. He expects you to:

- look ahead for a suitable place to stop
- check your mirror to see what is happening behind
- indicate to warn following drivers you are going to be slowing down to stop.

The examiner also expects you, as a driver, to select a safe place to stop at the side of the road.

Be careful you **don't**:

- block someone's driveway (they may want access)
- stop at a bus stop (in some areas the bus stop sign is fixed to a lamp post)
- stop opposite another vehicle
- stop opposite a side road.

When you stop, do so safely, remembering:

- use your mirrors
- inform following drivers that you intend to stop (indicate).

When you indicate be careful that you don't confuse other road users. For example, if there is a side road just before where you are going to stop, don't indicate too early – drivers waiting to come out of the side road may think you are turning into it, and pull out in front of you.

Always be aware of the rules on places where you must never stop, as given in *The Highway Code*.

When you have stopped the examiner will wait until you have applied your handbrake and put your gear lever into neutral before speaking.

MOVING OFF WHEN SAFE TO DO SO

When the examiner has explained what he wants you to do next or if
he just wants you to carry on driving he will probably say: 'Drive on
when you are ready, please.' Whenever you move away from the
kerb it is very important that you:

- check your mirror
- check over your shoulder
- pull away smoothly and safely.

This particularly applies when you are doing your reverse. On this
occasion the examiner will use an expression such as: 'Pull up just
before you reach the next road on the left, please.'

When you have stopped, if the examiner wants you to do a
'reverse round the corner', he will say something like: 'I should like
to reverse into this road on the left. Drive past it and stop, then back
in, and continue to drive in reverse gear for some distance, keeping
reasonably close to the kerb.'

The examiner will always ask you to stop before the road he wants
you to reverse into. This gives you an opportunity to:

- look into the road you are going to be reversing into
- stop in a position not too close to the kerb
- note what type of corner you will be reversing round (sharp,
  rounded, double).

Unfortunately this is where so many people forget the basic rules of
'moving off when safe to do so'. They are so busy thinking about the
imminent reverse that they forget the basic rules for 'moving off
safely'.

Remembering the basic rules

Always consider other road users by:

- using your mirrors correctly
- signalling if necessary
- cancelling your indicator if it has not cancelled automatically.

DOING THE EMERGENCY STOP

The examiner may ask you to do an emergency stop during the test,
this is now only carried out in one in three tests. If the examiner
wishes you to do an emergency stop he will ask you to 'pull up and
stop at a convenient place', he will then say something like: 'Very

shortly I shall ask you to stop as in an emergency. The signal will be like this. [He will then demonstrate the signal he will give, for example bang a book on the dashboard.] When I do that stop immediately and under full control, as though a child has run off the pavement.'

What the examiner is trying to convey is that when you stop it should be:

- quick
- controlled
- without locking the wheels and skidding.

Again I must emphasise the importance of moving away from the kerb safely after he has explained what he requires you to do.

The examiner will only ask you to do the emergency stop:

- in a quiet area
- when there are no vehicles behind
- on a reasonably level road.

Remember:

- keep two hands on the wheel until you have stopped completely
- keep the car in a straight line
- apply your footbrake before your clutch.

If you start to skid, which could happen if the road is wet, lift up your footbrake immediately and apply again, with a jerking action if necessary. Remember, after your emergency stop, the same procedure for pulling out from the kerb should be followed.

Many people stall the engine on the emergency stop; if you do so:

- don't worry
- apply your handbrake
- check you are in neutral
- start your engine again.

CHECKLIST

You should understand:

- what the examiner means when he asks you to 'follow the road ahead'
- stopping in a convenient place
- moving off safely
- what to be extra careful of when doing the emergency stop
- the type of expressions the examiner will use.

QUESTIONS AND ANSWERS

If I have to do a real emergency stop during my test, will the examiner still do this part of my test?

No. If a real emergency stop arises then the examiner will not need to test you on this exercise.

What should I do if after being asked to reverse round a corner, I note that a car is parking just where I would be going to reverse to?

Point it out to the examiner in case he cannot see it, he will ask you to carry on driving and will select another road.

Why does the examiner always ask you to stop before the road you are going to reverse into? Surely it would be more sensible to stop at the point where you are going to start your reverse?

Stopping before the target road is to help both the examiner and yourself. From your point of view it gives you an opportunity to:

- look at the road you are going to reverse into
- position yourself not too close to the kerb before you start to reverse.

Remember normally when you pull in you stop as near the kerb as you can. However, if you are going to reverse you need to position yourself about a third of a metre (a foot) from the kerb to give you room to manoeuvre the car without hitting the kerb. It is not a good idea to reverse along the gutter where bits of glass and other litter may have gathered.

From the examiner's point of view it gives him an opportunity to check that you:

- understand a safe place to stop
- stop correctly, using your mirrors and signal
- pull away from the kerb safely
- give clear signals which do not confuse other road users. For example, indicating too early when you are going to stop, thus misleading traffic emerging from the road on the left into thinking you are going to turn into that road.

CASE STUDIES

Scott's observation lets him down
Scott remembered that observation was very important when

driving, so throughout the test he looked well ahead, remembering to use his mirrors wisely. He was therefore surprised to discover he had failed on observation and stopping in an unsuitable place. He had unknowingly stopped at a bus stop.

After the test he said to his instructor, 'I was so busy being observant, and trying to look observant, I stopped using my common sense.'

His instructor seemed surprised that Scott would miss a bus stop sign.

'I didn't even notice it,' Scott said. 'It was a normal, fairly quiet tree-lined road. I checked I was not blocking a driveway, and there were no parked cars. However, I failed to notice the bus stop sign as it was on the lamp post I parked under.' He couldn't resist a smile, in spite of his disappointment, as he added, 'The examiner even asked, when I had stopped, if I was satisfied with my position. I had a look around and said yes!'

> Always check that you stop in a suitable place.
> Check for signs on lamp posts.

Christine mixes up her rights and lefts

Christine felt very nervous on her test, she didn't think she could afford more driving lessons if she failed.

'I would like you to take the next road on the left,' said the examiner.

Christine checked her mirror, indicated right and moved into position for a right turn. When the road was clear she completed her right turn, not noticing the examiner's slight surprised look.

'Could you take the next available road on your right, please?' As Christine listened to the examiner's request she was already checking her mirror and indicating left. She then turned into the next road on the left.

At the end of the test the examiner informed her, 'That is the end of the test and I'm pleased to tell you that you have passed. However,' he added, 'it might be a good idea if you sorted out your rights and lefts.'

> Examiners are only checking your ability to drive safely.
> If you turn the wrong way, providing you do so safely, giving the correct indications, it should not fail you on your test.

Sandra stops the test

Sandra was nervous on the day of the test. As the test progressed she could feel herself being so self critical that after about 15 minutes she stopped the car.

'I'm sorry,' she said to the examiner, 'I can't drive any more, you will have to drive back.'

The examiner was very understanding, and spoke with Sandra for a few minutes.

'Why not try again?' he said kindly. 'Just relax and enjoy the drive.'

After a moment's hesitation Sandra carried on driving, and to her surprise passed the test.

'There was nothing wrong with your driving,' the examiner explained afterwards. 'You were imagining faults and errors and working yourself into a failure state of mind. You demonstrated to me a very high standard of driving especially after you decided you were going to abandon the test.'

> Examiners are human and understand you feel nervous and self critical.

DISCUSSION POINTS

1. If you were an examiner how would you get a nervous candidate to relax?

2. Why do you think people get more nervous on a driving test than on most other tests?

3. If you knew someone who always got their rights and lefts mixed up when they were nervous, what would you suggest they do to help them remember on their driving test?

10
Thinking Positively at All Times

OVERCOMING COMMON PROBLEMS

The biggest problem for many people when taking the practical driving test is that while they are driving they are aware of the examiner sitting beside them. They feel the examiner is:

- watching every move
- noting every error
- waiting for them to make a mistake.

This kind of thinking results in the candidate:

- criticising themselves
- worrying throughout the test
- not concentrating properly on their driving.

They end up making mistakes and being unable to drive up to the standard required.

It is therefore very important that you:

- think positively at all times
- remember no one is perfect
- correct any mistakes and get on with your driving.

Understanding what to do if you stall

If you stall the car, which is a very natural thing to do, particularly if you are feeling a little tense or nervous, remember the drill:

- put your handbrake on
- check your gear lever is in neutral
- start the engine again.

The whole checking and re-starting procedure will only take a matter of a few seconds if you **do it immediately**.

If you start thinking about the fact you have stalled, and what the examiner might be thinking, you will find you are:

- wasting valuable seconds

- holding up traffic
- starting to get tense.

Sometimes people feel better if they say something, as they feel the silence when the engine stops seems to engulf them. A remark like: 'I seem to have stalled' as your start to do your drill, or 'I must be getting nervous' often helps to take away that awful feeling that perhaps you have made some unforgivable mistake.

Never try to start the engine while you are still in gear.

Remembering what to do if you start to roll back on an incline

The fear of rolling back on a hill or slope is a worry that most learners have. If you ever feel the car is starting to move backwards when you are moving away:

- stop immediately
- apply your handbrake
- check you are in first gear (not being in gear properly is one of the reasons people roll back, so put the gear lever back to neutral and then into first gear again)
- get your biting point again using your clutch and accelerator.

People often lose their biting point, particularly on a steep hill where they have pulled the handbrake on very hard, by losing the vital position on the clutch while they are releasing the handbrake. It is therefore a good idea when you lift the handbrake up a little to release it:

1. check you still have your biting point
2. release the handbrake
3. remember to apply a little extra pressure on your accelerator.

BREATHING CORRECTLY TO HELP EASE NERVOUS TENSION

Everyone at sometime in their life feels a little nervous or apprehensive. Going to the dentist or flying are two events that cause many people to get very worried and tense. However, taking the practical driving test is perhaps one of the major events that produces more apprehension and nervousness, causing candidates to act very much out of character. If this happens to you:

- take a deep breath

- hold it for a few seconds
- slowly breathe out.

This normally helps as it introduces extra oxygen to your body, clearing your head and helping you to think more clearly.
If you feel this does not help:

- look for a suitable place to stop your car
- stop safely
- remember to use your mirrors correctly.

Once you have stopped:

- explain to the examiner why you have stopped
- wind down the window a little
- take a couple more deep breaths
- try sucking a mint.

After a minute you should feel a little easier and be able to continue your test safely.

OBSERVING OTHER ROAD USERS AT ALL TIMES

It is amazing how often people blame the actions of another driver, or a car parked in the wrong place, for their failure to pass a driving test, forgetting that the skill of driving lies in the ability to:

- anticipate the actions of others
- look well ahead
- act responsibly on what is happening all around.

By the time you take your test you should be confident in your ability to drive and be developing the right attitude towards other road users.
It is always important to remember that no one is a perfect driver, even the best drivers sometimes make mistakes.

> Watch other drivers. Make allowances for any mistakes
> they may make.

This is one of the many reasons you never travel too close to the vehicle in front. You must always:

- be prepared to slow down or stop if necessary
- be tolerant at all times.

On a driving test one of the most common mistakes is to keep thinking about something that has happened. Remember in driving it is important to:

- forget what has happened because:
  - that has finished
  - you can't change it

- look well ahead (however, always be aware of what is happening behind you)

- plan ahead:
  - remembering to be in the right gear
  - at the right time
  - in the right position on the road.

When on your driving test be particularly observant if you notice a learner driver. Be prepared for them to make mistakes.

OBEYING THE RULES OF *THE HIGHWAY CODE*

It is very important that drivers are aware of the rules as laid down in *The Highway Code* and act on them. As a relatively new driver you will have studied *The Highway Code* thoroughly and know the rules and regulations. However, many drivers have been driving for years and unfortunately don't always keep up with changing rules and regulations. So be prepared at all times for mistakes by other road users.

Remember that a road user is not only someone in a car; you must pay particular attention to:

- motorcyclists who may come up quickly on either side of your car

- pedal cyclists who may wobble, and so need extra consideration and plenty of clearance when you pass them

- children who may rush into the road without thinking

- pedestrians who do not always understand the speed of traffic, or the rules and regulations

- horse riders. They require you to show extra care and consideration, as horses are easily frightened. Never pass them at speed, sound your horn, or rev the engine. Give them plenty of room.

The *Code*'s ten commandments

The Highway Code is the bible of the road user; you could even say it has its own ten commandments:

1. Do not drive under the influence of alcohol.
2. Do not drive under the influence of drugs.
3. Do not drive when you are angry or upset.
4. Drive in the correct place in the road.
5. Know your traffic signs and act on them.
6. Keep to the speed limits.
7. Never stop or park where it is forbidden to do so.
8. Ensure your vehicle is in a roadworthy condition.
9. Have your vehicle insured and taxed at all times.
10. Show consideration, patience and thoughtfulness to other road users at all times.

You must always remember to:

* listen for the sound of any emergency vehicle
* look as far ahead as you can
* sense a danger before you get involved.

HAVING CONFIDENCE TO TAKE CHARGE INSIDE YOUR VEHICLE

During the time you have been learning to drive, there has always been someone at hand to advise and warn you what you need to do, or answer any query. Your driving test is therefore the first opportunity you have of being **solely** in charge of a vehicle. The examiner is merely an observer.

Try to think of the examiner as a non-driving person who is directing you to a certain point. He knows where he is going; however, you as the driver have to make the decisions on how to drive safely on the way there.

If you are driving a small car, and the examiner is a large person or has heavy clothing on, you may find that you cannot use the gears or handbrake without touching some part of his clothing, which is making you uneasy. If this happens:

* ask him politely to move a little, or move the offending item such as a trailing jacket that is causing you a problem.

Don't continue the test if you feel uncomfortable and squashed while driving; also the examiner would be most concerned if you did not speak up about this until after the test.

Coping with wet weather on your test

Remember, if it starts to rain, use your windscreen wipers. Because they are nervous and concentrating on what they are doing, many learner drivers wait until they can hardly see before remembering to put on their wipers, which is very dangerous as their vision is cut down considerably by this time.

> Double check you know where the wipers are and how to use them before going to meet your examiner.

It has been known for people never to have had to use the wipers until their test, and then panic as they cannot find the switch.

If the windows start to steam up:

- switch on the fan, ensuring the air is directed at the windscreen
- wind down your window a little.

If you find because of the weather you have difficulty seeing out of the side and back windows:

- stop in a suitable place
- clean the windows (inside and outside if necessary).

Never carry on driving if your windows are steamed up.

If the fan is on, and the noise is distracting you, turn it down, or off if necessary.

Making the correct decisions while doing your manoeuvres

If while you are doing the reverse a car starts to come along the road you are reversing into, stop, and drive forward if necessary.

If while you are doing the turn in the road a car or cyclist comes along the road, stop, and assess what they intend to do (are they going to pass you or wait). **Never wave anyone on.**

Remember, **you**:

- are in charge of the vehicle
- have to make all the decisions within the vehicle
- must use your initiative and common sense at all times.

CHECKLIST

You should now understand:

- how to cope if you stall

- how breathing can help ease nervous tension
- the importance of observing other road users at all times
- how to observe the rules of *The Highway Code*
- that during the test you are in charge of the vehicle and what happens within it.

QUESTIONS AND ANSWERS

I like to have music while I am driving – it relaxes me and stops me feeling nervous. Can I play my favourite tape during my test?

Loud music would not be a good idea; however, I am sure the examiner would have no objections if you played it very quietly. As your first consideration is to your passenger, it would be courteous to ask if he would object if you played your tape quietly throughout the test. Always remember the examiner is working and has a job to do, so he must not be distracted.

I know it must sound very silly, but I am worried about what to do if the car breaks down during my driving test – if it had a puncture, for example, or I stalled the car and it wouldn't start again because of some mechanical fault?

Normally when someone is taking the test, the person who has been teaching them makes sure that the car is in good mechanical order. However, in the unlikely event of the car breaking down the examiner would abandon the test. He would ask for the keys and take them back to the test centre to return to your instructor. You would need to apply for another test. Unfortunately you would not have your test fee refunded.

Is it true that if you stall the car more than twice it is an automatic failure?

Examiners realise that candidates are normally a little apprehensive, and therefore are more inclined to stall the car, and make allowances for this, providing that you carry out the correct procedure after you have stalled (handbrake on and into neutral before starting the engine). A stall could be compared to a sneeze – it is an event that is not planned, it happens to everyone, so you just sort it out then get on with the job. However, if nearly every time you stopped you stalled, then the examiner would presume that you had a problem with using your foot pedals correctly.

CASE STUDIES

Liz nearly panics

Liz felt she was doing quite well on her driving test. It was a sunny day and she was enjoying having the windows open. She had done the turn in the road and was pleased with her reverse park. They were heading back to the test centre when Liz noticed a bee on the back window. For a moment she felt panic, then forcing herself to be calm, she quickly checked her mirror, indicated, pulled to a halt and stopped the engine.

'I'm sorry,' she said to the examiner, as she started to get out of the car. 'I'm allergic to bee stings, and there is a bee in the car.'

The examiner opened the window, and within a minute the insect flew away. The examiner said, 'Perhaps it might be a good idea to keep the windows closed so no more bees are tempted to join us.'

As Liz, who was feeling quite flustered, put on her seat belt ready to carry on with her test, the examiner advised her to take her time and drive only when she felt ready.

Liz regained her composure and finished the test, and was delighted to hear that she had passed.

> When things go wrong it is quite in order to stop as long as you do so correctly and with consideration for other drivers.

Tom makes a decision

The day Tom took his driving test it was pouring with rain. By the time the examiner and Tom got into the car, they were both fairly wet and within a few minutes of driving the windows started to steam up.

'If you don't mind,' Tom said to the examiner, 'I'm going to pull in and stop up the road here, and clean the windows.'

When he stopped Tom used the cloth which was kept in the car to wipe over all the inside windows, then quickly cleaned the outside of the side windows.

Back in the car, he opened his window slightly, and once the engine was started made sure the air vents were directed at the windscreen. He also turned the fan on a little.

As Tom looked towards the examiner he noticed he was smiling. 'That was a good idea,' he said. 'This weather always causes problems with vision.' Tom felt confident and relaxed as he continued with his test, which he passed.

> Always make sure you have good all round vision. Keep a cloth handy in case you need to clean steamed up windows.

Phyllis talks her way through the test

Phyllis was nearly 50 when she started to learn to drive. She had always thought she was too nervous to learn, but after her husband became ill she had had to learn to drive as they lived in a very isolated area. She had found an understanding driving instructor who had taught her carefully. She also read books on driving, and each night in bed she went over what she had learned that day.

On the day of the test Phyllis felt more apprehensive than nervous, and was delighted that her examiner was an elderly man.

As she checked over her shoulder to pull away from the kerb, she found herself saying, 'You know it's so important to check over your shoulder before moving off.'

As the test progressed Phyllis repeatedly thought out loud: 'The car behind is far too close, I wish people would realise the danger of driving so close,' or 'Look at those children, you really have to watch out for them – they might just run into the road.'

Phyllis continued to utter her little gems of wisdom as she drove around the test route. At the end of the test the examiner was pleased to inform Phyllis that she had passed. He later told her instructor what a conscientious driver Phyllis was.

> Sometimes you may feel happier if you talk to yourself during your test.

DISCUSSION POINTS

1. Besides taking deep breaths, what other ways can you think of to help you when you are feeling nervous?

2. *The Highway Code* is updated every few years. What ways can you think of to ensure that all drivers and road users are aware of any changes?

3. Do you think that taking a driving test on a wet day is more difficult than on a nice dry sunny day? What are the advantages and disadvantages of driving in either?

11
Coping with Hazards

KNOWING WHAT TO DO WHEN ENCOUNTERING UNEXPECTED HAZARDS

However well you have prepared for your driving test, and however well you may know the town or city where you are taking the test, an unexpected hazard, one you have not previously encountered, can cause you to make wrong decisions, even panic. For example:

- a road closed which had been open earlier in the day
- road markings changed giving priority to a different road
- someone parked illegally
- parked vehicles blocking your view as you try to enter a road
- traffic lights not working
- a demonstration or march blocking the road.

These are just a few of the unexpected hazards which can cause even the most confident learner to make a bad decision. Normally the examiners will try to avoid this kind of hazard. However, sometimes things happen on the roads which the examiner has no warning of.

If we look at each of the example hazards separately, you will see that most things can be sorted out without any problems. Remember once you have passed your test you will have to sort out any of these problems, safely and correctly, yourself.

The road is closed ahead of you
If a road is closed for any reason, there is normally a road sign with an arrow to show which way the traffic now has to go. This is all part of 'reading the road correctly'. You should notice all road signs and act on them.

The road markings are changed and the road you are on is no longer the priority road
Just drive normally, remembering to obey the sign and give way at the junction. Watch carefully for traffic on the other road which may

not have noticed the change in priority.

A lorry is unloading near a pedestrian crossing
Slow right down, change to a lower gear, indicate, pass the lorry slowly being prepared to stop if there are any pedestrians on the crossing. Keep a careful eye on traffic behind you, which may be travelling too close.

Parked vehicles block your vision as you try to pull out from a side road
This perhaps is one of the most likely hazards which you may encounter. The first thing to remember is to stop if there's a stop line. If it's a give way junction then you can continue slowly forward. Remember:

- look for pedestrians who may be crossing the road you are on

- look on both sides for cyclists who are travelling on the inside of traffic on the main road

- creep forward very slowly, using your clutch to control the speed of the car

- when the front of your car is level with the offside of the parked cars, stop and check again (remember you are still in a safe position as cars take a course to overtake a row of parked cars (see Figure 9)).

- creep forward a little more if necessary to improve your view.

Never try saying a prayer and pulling out (this would most likely cause an accident).

– Be **patient**
– Be **observant**
– Be **prepared** to move out when you can see the road is clear.

You come to some traffic lights and they are not working
Normally the police try to control the traffic when the lights go out of order. However, you may arrive at the lights just after the fault has occurred.

- Look to see if there is a secondary sign by the lights which informs you if you are on a main or secondary road. Some lights may have a give way sign by them. If you are on the minor road, treat the junction as a give way or stop. If you are on the major road proceed with caution.

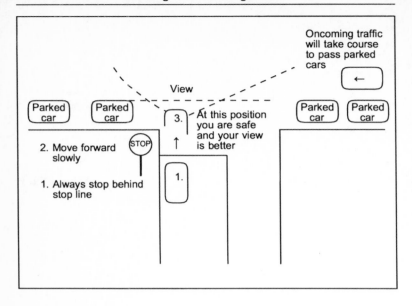

Fig. 9. Pulling out when parked cars obscure your view.

- If there are no indications which road has priority, look carefully at the other traffic, proceed slowly, observing all around at all times.

- **Never panic**.

There is some kind of demonstration or march in front of you
Slow down and keep well back. The examiner will most likely ask you to turn off the road somewhere, or wait until the march changes direction.

Remember any unexpected hazard requires a little more thought and care, so as soon as you see something unexpected change to a lower gear to enable you to assess the situation better.

DEALING WITH INCLEMENT WEATHER

Weather conditions affect our driving far more than many people realise. Different weather conditions not only change people's attitude to driving, but also affect other road users like cyclists and pedestrians.

For example, when the weather is sunny and warm people tend to feel relaxed, pedestrians are more likely to stroll into the road, cyclists wobble as they chat to other cyclists, and motorists open windows and enjoy the feel of cool air as they speed along, often going far too fast.

When it is wet, however, pedestrians put their heads down, dash across roads, and motorists have much more to think about. Windows get steamed up. Vision is reduced. Wipers have to be used.

Coping with rain

If it rains during your test:

- remember to put on your wipers
- clean any windows which have steamed up when you are stopped
- keep your window open a little to help clear condensation
- remember that your stopping distances are increased in wet weather, so keep well back from the vehicle in front
- watch out for pedestrians who may dash across the road without looking properly.

Coping with snow

If during your test it starts to snow:

- slow down by easing your foot gently off the accelerator
- switch on your wipers
- switch on your lights
- be extra careful with all your controls
- don't brake suddenly, use your brake carefully.

Coping with fog

If during the test a thick fog comes down:

- switch on your dipped headlights
- slow right down – you must drive according to your vision
- be extra watchful for other vehicles which may have defective or no lights on
- keep near to the centre line: there may be cyclists near the kerb
- wind your window down a little so you can hear any traffic.

Normally if it becomes very foggy, or starts to snow, the examiner will abandon the test, and you will be given another appointment without extra charge.

FEELING TOO NERVOUS TO CARRY ON

It is an unusual person who does not feel a little apprehensive and nervous when taking their practical driving test. It is one of the rare times in our life when someone is watching our moves carefully to judge our ability. A person who is normally nervous is used to this feeling, and has found ways to cope with it. However, a normally confident person who suddenly feels nervous is more likely to find it very difficult to cope with the situation.

If you feel you cannot carry on driving safely:

- stop the car in a suitable place
- explain the situation to the examiner
- have a sweet
- try taking deep breaths.

If you then feel a little better try driving on. Remember during your driving life you are going to have to drive safely while experiencing all kinds of emotions, for example

- grief
- anger
- happiness
- excitement.

If you still feel you cannot carry on with your test, tell the examiner, who will then abandon the test. You will have to apply and pay for another test. I would recommend that you take extra lessons to build up your confidence, to enable you to drive safely whatever state your personal emotions are in.

CHECKLIST

You should now:

- be able to make the right decisions if you encounter an unexpected hazard

- know how to drive correctly in any weather conditions during your test

- know what to do if you feel too nervous to carry on driving during your test

- be aware that your driving examiner is not a monster, but another normal person who is trying to do a very difficult job.

QUESTIONS AND ANSWERS

If it is very wet during the test and I skid on the emergency stop, will the examiner fail me?

The idea of the emergency stop is to check that your reactions and control of the vehicle are such that in a real emergency you could stop the vehicle quickly, and under control. Emergencies do not only happen in good, dry weather conditions – in fact you are more likely to encounter them when it is wet and icy. It is therefore important that you know how to stop quickly regardless of the weather.

If you do an emergency stop in the wet and you feel you are going to skid, just lift your foot quickly off the foot brake and apply it again. This pumping action of the brake prevents the wheels locking, and ensures a smooth, safe, quick stop. Remember to always keep two hands firmly on the wheel until the car has stopped completely.

I find chewing gum helps me not only to feel less nervous, but also to concentrate better. I have been told that examiners object to people who chew gum the whole time. Is this correct?

The examiner is there to test your ability to drive safely. He would have no objection to you chewing your gum, providing of course you do it quietly and discreetly. It would be courteous at the start of the test to say something like, 'I hope you won't mind if I chew gum, it helps me concentrate'.

I am under five foot tall, and when driving I have two cushions, one under me and one behind me, to enable me to see properly and to reach the foot controls. My friend told me that you are not allowed to drive with loose cushions on the seat. Will the examiner object to me driving with all these extra cushions?

The examiner will have no objections to you driving with your cushions, provided you drive safely, and with full control of the car. It is worth noting that some car manufacturers seem to cater for the very small and the very tall. It is therefore worthwhile when you buy a vehicle for yourself to look at all the different makes. Failing this you can have adjustments made to your seat and pedals to make it easier and more comfortable for you to drive. However, during your driving test your cushions, which you have been using throughout your lessons, will be quite acceptable.

CASE STUDIES

Duncan follows his own route

Although it had been raining hard throughout his driving test, Duncan felt he was driving well. On the road back to the test centre he caught up with a bus. Keeping well behind it, he remembered to notice whether any of the passengers stood up to ring the bell. 'It will give you a clue that the bus is going to stop shortly', his instructor had told him. As the bus turned to the left, Duncan followed it.

'Turn right.' The examiner's voice, a little sharper than usual, interrupted Duncan's thoughts.

At the end of the test the examiner queried why Duncan had followed the bus into a street marked 'Buses only'.

'I thought you asked me to turn there', replied Duncan.

The examiner smiled as he replied, 'I did not ask you to turn anywhere – there was no need, you were on the direct road to return to this test centre.'

Duncan had to re-sit his driving test.

> Listen carefully to the examiner's directions.

Jane makes a decision

During her test Jane was driving downhill along a busy dual carriageway. Up to that moment she had not been happy with her driving. She knew she had made a couple of little errors, she had even stalled twice. As she entered the dual carriageway she had an excellent view down the hill, and she noticed a large lorry appeared to have stopped at the bottom of the hill. The traffic behind the lorry was starting to build up, she could see indicators flashing as drivers tried to pull over to the right hand lane, but were prevented from doing so because of the traffic moving quickly in that lane.

'Better change lanes now, while it is easier to do so,' thought Jane, as she checked her mirrors, indicated and smoothly moved into the right hand lane of the dual carriageway.

She was glad she had done so, as she passed the stationery lorry and the long tail back of traffic stuck behind it.

At the end of the test the examiner informed her she had passed the test and complimented her on her forward planning while driving down the dual carriageway.

> Look well ahead and plan ahead when driving.

Janice meets a problem

Janice had just finished her turn in the road and was driving away when she noticed a van reversing towards her fairly fast. There was a car coming towards her on the other side, but nothing behind her.

She stopped the car and reversed away from the van, which stopped, and the driver jumped out and disappeared into a building.

'He didn't even look,' she said in surprise. 'If I had been just a little further ahead he would have backed straight into me.'

'You seemed to handle it very well,' said the examiner encouragingly. 'Drive on when you are ready.'

Janice completed her test and passed.

> Always be on the look out for the unexpected. Remember the only person you can trust on the road is yourself.

DISCUSSION POINTS

1. How do you cope with bad driving you encounter?

2. Do you know your minimum stopping distances? Have you any idea of the actual distance you would travel if you had to stop suddenly when driving at 50 mph in wet weather?

3. When driving at night it is difficult to see pedestrians wearing dark coloured clothing. Do you think that all pedestrians should wear a reflective band at night?

12
Hearing the Results of your Tests

RECEIVING THE RESULTS OF THE THEORY TEST

You will receive the results of your theory test within seven to ten days. However, during busy holiday periods, it may take a couple of days longer. It is possible at certain test centres to receive your results the same day if you pay an extra fee.

If you have passed
Well done, you now have the basic grounding to make a good driver.

- Use the knowledge you have learned so far and improve on it.
- Put it into practice as you prepare for your practical test.
- Keep all the books you studied for reference. (They can prove very helpful if you have a query, or if any aspect of driving worries you.)

If you have not passed
Do not get too disheartened, perhaps you were not fully prepared for the test. Although you can apply immediately to retake the test, it would be advisable to:

- study the relevant literature further
- find the questions you were asked on your paper and study the answer given
- look at the various questions and understand why a certain answer is correct
- discuss the questions and answers with your friends and family.

When you feel confident you understand the questions and answers:

- apply to take the theory test again
- don't give up.

LISTENING TO WHAT THE EXAMINER TELLS YOU

At the end of the practical driving test the examiner will tell you if you have passed or failed. Unfortunately most people find that whatever the outcome, they have difficulty taking in what the examiner says because they are either excited if they have passed or, disappointed and unhappy if they have failed.

However, the examiner will be trying to give you valuable and useful information so do try to listen and understand what is being said to you.

If you have passed
You will be given:

- a pass certificate
- a copy of the driving test report which will show any minor faults which have been marked during the test (nobody drives perfectly and even if you pass you will have made a few minor mistakes).

You should:

- listen carefully to what the examiner says
- speak to your instructor about what is marked on the sheet.

It is important you are aware of these faults, and make every effort to improve your standard of driving, otherwise you could end up involved in an accident.

If you don't pass
The examiner will:

- explain briefly why you haven't passed
- give you a driving test report form which will show the faults marked during the test (see Figure 10).

Listen carefully to what he says, as it will help you understand the serious mistakes you have made which could have caused a danger on the road. However, the examiner can only tell you briefly why the items are listed, he has no time to discuss them in detail.

On the reverse side of your driving test report form you will find an explanation of the markings used by the examiner, which clarify the degree of fault.

/	signifies a minor fault, which will not result in failure
X	signifies a serious fault, and
D	indicates a dangerous fault. Committing either of these faults will result in failure.

Driving Test Report

Candidate's Name

Vehicle Type   Registration No.

Driver Number

1(a). Eyesight   1(b). Highway Code (Categories F/G/H)

2. Precautions

3. Control :-
- accelerator
- clutch
- gears
- footbrake
- handbrake
- steering
- balance m/c

4. Move away :-
- safely
- under control

5. Emergency stop :- promptness
- control
- making proper use of front brake (m/c)

6. Reverse to left or right :- control
- observation

7. Turn in the road / 'U' turn (m/c) :- control
- observation

8. Reverse parking :- control
- observation

R C

9. Use of mirrors / rear observation (m/c) well before :-
- signalling
- changing direction
- changing speed

10. Give appropriate signals :-
- where necessary
- correctly
- properly timed

11. Response to signs and signals :-
- traffic signs
- road markings
- traffic lights
- traffic controllers
- other road users

12. Use of speed

13. Following distance

14. Maintain progress by :-
- driving at an appropriate speed
- avoiding undue hesitation

15. Junctions :-
- approach speed
- observation
- turning right
- turning left
- cutting corners

16. Judgement when :-
- overtaking
- meeting traffic
- crossing traffic

17. Positioning :-
- normal driving
- lane discipline

18. Clearance to obstructions

19. Pedestrian crossings

20. Position for normal stops

21. Awareness and planning

22. Ancillary controls

Total driving faults :-

23. Result of test   Pass   Fail

Extended test

Examiner's signature

Examiner's name

Authorised by the Secretary of State to conduct driving tests

Test Terminated in the Interest of Public Safety		
Test Terminated at Request of Candidate		
Examiner Took Action	Verbal	Physical
Oral Explanation Given	Yes	No

DRIVING STANDARDS AGENCY
"Safe driving for life"
awarded for excellence

ADI Number	Category
Test Centre	
Date	M
Time of Test	F

Fig. 10. Driving test report.

You will obviously feel very disappointed if you don't pass your driving test, even angry. This is a natural reaction after working and studying so hard, often for many months. However, it is important that you:

- study the driving test report form
- refer to the relevant sections in the Driving Standards Agency book *The Driving Test*
- show your copy of the driving test report form to your instructor
- try to get as much practice as possible before your next driving test to improve all aspects of your driving
- take your next test as soon as you feel confident that you have rectified your mistakes.

If you feel unhappy about the way the test was conducted, and believe it was not carried out according to the government's regulations, you can appeal to the Department of Transport. However, the examiner's decision can't be changed, and you would still have to take another test.

KNOWING WHAT TO DO AFTER YOUR DRIVING TEST

If you have failed the test, build on the knowledge that you have learned during the test. Remember it is far better to have more tuition and learn as much as you can while you can, as once you have passed the test it is presumed you know all the answers.

For those who have passed as well as for those who have failed it is now important while the test is still fresh in your mind to:

- study the driving test report form the examiner gave you
- discuss the faults with your instructor
- try to understand why and where you made the errors shown
- improve your driving standard.

Sadly a lot of accidents involve new drivers who do not have much driving experience, particularly on motorways. It is therefore a good idea to:

- **improve your driving** by building on the basic skills you now have
- **gain valuable experience** by observation and driving on a variety of different roads.

The 'Pass Plus' scheme
One way of doing this is by taking further instruction on the 'Pass Plus' scheme which has been developed by the Department of Transport in partnership with the insurance industry. The scheme

has been developed to:

- improve driving skills in areas where you may have little experience
- reduce the risk of your being involved in a road accident
- introduce you to motorway driving in a safe manner
- show you a driving style which is both positive and safe
- help you gain quality driving experience safely.

Many people feel that once they have passed their driving test, they are a driver and will not need further instruction. Passing your initial driving tests is only the start of being a good driver. You now have permission by law to drive alone, but it takes a long time, even years, to become a really confident and good driver.

CHECKLIST

You should feel confident about taking your driving tests and know:

- how you will receive the results
- that the examiner will pass you even if you have made minor errors
- how to cope if you fail
- that you should take more lessons whether you pass or fail
- the importance of the 'Pass Plus' scheme.

QUESTIONS AND ANSWERS

As you no longer need to wait a calendar month between driving tests, is it a good idea to retake my practical test straight away if I fail?

It depends very much on why you failed your test. For some candidates another test in a short while is a good idea. However, if a candidate becomes so nervous without his normal instructor there to advise him that he makes serious errors, than I would suggest that extra lessons would help increase confidence and improve the standard of driving.

I have heard that people who have taken more than one test are often better drivers in the long run than people who has passed first time.

No survey has been carried out. However, if you have had to work extra hard to gain a qualification you tend to value it more. Thus the person who passes a driving test at the first try often thinks it was easy and that they know it all. However, if you fail a driving test, and have to go through the disappointment and anxiety of taking it again, not only do you gain extra experience between tests, but you appreciate the hard work, skill and knowledge that goes to make a good driver.

I think the idea behind the 'Pass Plus' scheme is a good one, but I am a student, and I expect many people like me feel that they have already laid out a lot of money for the initial driving lessons, and just cannot afford to pay out any extra. Is it really worth the extra expense?

Driving is a skill and unfortunately a large number of accidents involve new inexperienced drivers. To pay out a little extra to ensure you can cope with the more hazardous conditions you will be meeting on roads, particularly motorways, is a sound investment in your future. Without it you may not have the knowledge to cope with an emergency which may arise. You could ask your relatives to contribute towards the 'Pass Plus' course as a Christmas or birthday present. Moreover, in this case, particularly being a student, you could save money. Insurance companies who are taking part in the scheme are giving reduced rates on insurance.

CASE STUDIES

Joan gets over emotional

Joan has always been a very emotional person, inclined to burst into tears. On the day of her driving test she felt confident, although a little nervous. However, she made a serious error and when the examiner informed her she had not passed she dissolved into tears.

As the instructor drove her home, Joan explained between sobs that she was a very emotional person, and any disappointment affected her in this way.

A few weeks later Joan re-took the test, and this time she passed. However, her instructor was horrified to find when he approached the car that once again Joan was sobbing as though her heart would break. Once again she explained that 'any great joy or disappointment affected her in this way'.

On this occasion her instructor not only had to take her home, but had to wait with her until she calmed down. Just as he felt it was safe to leave, a next door neighbour called round to see how Joan had got on in the test. As she said 'How did you get on then? Did you pass?' Joan immediately burst into tears again.

Her instructor made his escape, amazed that anyone could become so emotional not only at a disappointment, but also when they were successful.

> People can have very intense reactions to their test results.

Lucy gets angry

Lucy was confident on the day of her test. She had worked hard at learning to drive, the same way as she had worked hard for all her exams.

'People only fail tests or exams because they do not study hard enough,' she used to say. 'I have no sympathy with people who fail any exam or test.'

During her test she failed to observe an unmarked crossroad just after she had done her reverse. When the examiner failed her she was furious.

'He failed me deliberately because I'm a woman,' she told her instructor angrily. 'It was a quiet area, a very narrow road and no one was coming; I think he was trying to trick me.'

Her instructor explained that if a motorbike or even a cyclist had been coming she would have caused an accident. Lucy would not listen and went away feeling angry and cheated.

Before she took her next test she had a lesson and said to the instructor, 'I am sorry about the way I behaved after the test. The examiner was right to fail me. After I had time to think things over I realised in a way he did me a good turn.' Her instructor looked inquiring.

'Yes,' Lucy continued. 'I realise now even the smallest road could be a potential danger, and I have to be aware of any unmarked roads where no priority is given. I hadn't failed anything before and I was always very unsympathetic to anyone who failed. In fact I was quite horrid to my friends who failed their GCSE exams. I know now how they felt; I also realise that, however hard you study or try, sometimes there is an X factor which can cause you to fail.'

Later as they drove along she added, 'Failing that test has taught me a valuable lesson. I think I will be a lot more understanding in the future when I hear of people who fail.'

Lucy passed her next test.

> Failing a test can often be a lesson in itself.

Philip goes too slow

Philip was a very confident driver. 'Too confident,' his father used to say to his mother after a practice drive. 'He drives far too fast, he needs to slow down a little.' As the day of his driving test drew near his father became increasingly angry about Philip's excessive use of speed.

'If you don't keep to the speed limit you will fail your test and could cause an accident,' his father said on the day of the test. 'You're not being tested to see if you are fit for the Monte Carlo rally, just to see if you are safe to handle this car on the road.'

As Philip got into the car with his examiner he remembered what his father had said.

'No speeding,' he thought. 'If I keep to 25 miles an hour that should do the trick.'

Throughout the test he drove carefully and slowly and was amazed when at the end of the test the examiner not only failed him but seemed irritated.

'You were a danger on the road, driving at that speed the whole time,' he said. 'You even did your pull outs in slow motion. I suggest you have a little more practice in driving according to the road and traffic conditions.'

When Philip told his parents what had happened he was surprised and a little hurt when his father started to laugh.

'Serves you right,' he said. 'Now will you listen when I talk about speed limits? Driving is not about getting in a car and putting your foot down, it's about observation, consideration and handling the car correctly in all types of road and traffic conditions.'

Philip failed one more test before he eventually passed.

> It is just as dangerous to go too slow as it is to go too fast.
> You should always drive according to road and traffic conditions.

DISCUSSION POINTS

1. Why is it just as dangerous to drive too slow as to drive too fast?

2. Do you think smoking in vehicles should be banned as it involves driving with only one hand on the wheel?

3. Once you have learned to drive and passed your test, at first you still feel a little apprehensive driving alone. Do you think that new drivers should display a 'P' (for probationer) on the car, to inform other road users that they are not yet fully experienced?

Glossary

Approved Driving Instructor. A driving instructor who has passed a 90-minute written exam, passed a strict driving test, reached a high standard in instruction and is checked regularly by the Driving Standards Agency.

Attitude. Behaviour towards other road users. Drivers should be tolerant, understanding and observant at all times.

Blind spot. An area where your vision is obscured by part of your vehicle or an object outside your vehicle: for example, a tree or a person standing on the pavement. You should always be aware of where the blind spots are and remember 'a second look can be your lifesaver'.

Complex questions. A question which has more than one possible answer.

Cockpit checks. The five basic checks you must make before starting the engine (see Chapter 5).

Clutch control. The balance between your clutch and accelerator which helps you to move off smoothly and to move slowly under control when manoeuvring or in traffic jams without stalling.

Department of Transport. Government department that controls all matters relating to transport.

Driving Standards Agency (DSA). Executive agency of the Department of Transport whose aim is to promote road safety through the advancement of driving standards.

Examiner. A person approved by the DSA to conduct driving tests.

Forward planning. Looking well ahead and anticipating what actions are needed.

Give way lines. Dotted lines across the end of a road, indicating that you are approaching a major road.

Hazard. A danger requiring more care and skill than usual.

Highway Code. Booklet produced by the Department of Transport giving road traffic law, advice and rules for all road users.

Kangaroo. When loss of balance of clutch and accelerator causes the car to jump (see Chapter 6).

Manoeuvres. Movement such as reversing, turning in the road or parking which require more observation and skill in handling your vehicle.

Practical test. The driving test taken with an examiner in your car.

Provisional licence. A temporary licence which allows you to practise driving with a suitable person accompanying you.

Pass Plus. A course of post-test lessons with an approved instructor to introduce you to motorway and other aspects of more skilled driving.

Reading the road. The skill of looking and planning ahead.

Stall. When the engine stops because you made an error with your footwork.

Stop lines. Unbroken lines at the end of a road which mean you must stop before crossing them.

Test routes. Routes which examiners usually use when conducting a driving test.

Theory test. The written part of the driving test.

Theory Test Pass Certificate. The certificate which is issued by the DSA to prove you have passed your theory test.

Turn in the road. Turning the car round in a road so you are facing the opposite way (formerly known as the three point turn).

Further Reading

Driving Manual, Driving Standards Agency (HMSO).
Know your Traffic Signs, Department of Transport (HMSO).
Teaching someone to Drive, Angela Oatridge (How To Books).
Test yourself papers for the Driving Theory Test, Driving Standards Agency (HMSO).
The Driving Test, Driving Standards Agency (HMSO).
The Motorcycle Manual, Driving Standards Agency (HMSO).
The Official Theory Test, Driving Standard Agency (HMSO).

Note:

Driving rules change regularly, therefore it is important that you use the latest edition of any books or driving regulations.

Index

accelerator, 56
age, 51
anticipation, 14
appearance, 41
attitude, 23

blind spots, 55, 63

clutch, 56, 69
cockpit checks, 49, 55, 77
cyclists, 66, 69

documents, 23, 35, 36, 42
Driving Manual, 22

emergency stop, 80–81, 98–99
examiner, 47–50, 52–64, 77–81
eyesight, 35, 48–49

failing the test, 19, 102, 103–105
forward planning, 61–62

gears, 63, 64, 65
give way lines, 63, 65

hazards, 94–96
Highway Code, 13, 88, 89
hills, 44, 86

instruction, 12, 19, 33

kangarooing, 56, 60

language, 17, 18, 30

manoeuvres, 69–74
mirrors, 55, 58, 80
Motorcycling Manual, 22

nerves, 43, 44–45, 47–48, 51–54,
   85–87, 97–98
number plate, reading a, 35, 48–49

observation, 14, 65, 68, 70, 87

parking, 42, 72
Pass Plus, 105–106, 107
positive thinking, 40, 41, 72–73, 75,
   85
practical test, 11–12, 23, 40
proof of identity, 23–24, 31–32

results, 101–103
reverse park, 70, 72, 75–76
reversing, 69–71, 73–74, 80, 82, 90
road signs, 25, 27, 62–64, 66

safety skills, 15
stalling, 56–57, 85–86
starting the engine, 55
stop lines, 63, 65
stopping, 79

technical skills, 15
theory test, 11, 21–30, 102
traffic signs, 25, 27, 62–63
turn in the road, 70, 74, 90

weather, 40, 92, 96–97